AMERICA The BEAUTIFUL
KENTUCKY

By Sylvia McNair

Consultants

Helen Worthington, Evaluation Coordinator Chapter I Programs, Kentucky Department of Education

Lucinda Sanders, Chairman, Social Studies Department, Danville Independent Schools

Mattie E. Clay, School Library/Media Specialist, Jefferson County Public Schools

James C. Klotter, State Historian and General Editor, Kentucky Historical Society

Robert L. Hillerich, Ph.D., Bowling Green State University, Bowling Green, Ohio

CHILDRENS PRESS ®
CHICAGO

Churchill Downs, Louisville

Project Editor: Joan Downing
Assistant Editor: Shari Joffe
Design Director: Margrit Fiddle
Typesetting: Graphic Connections, Inc.
Engraving: Liberty Photoengraving

Childrens Press®, Chicago
Copyright ©1988 by Regensteiner Publishing Enterprises, Inc.
All rights reserved. Published simultaneously in Canada.
Printed in the United States of America.
   3 4 5 6 7 8 9 10 R 97 96 95 94 93 92 91 90 89

Library of Congress Cataloging-in-Publication Data

McNair, Sylvia.
  America the beautiful. Kentucky.

  (America the beautiful state books)
  Includes index.
  Summary: Introduces the geography, history,
government, economy, culture, famous sites and
people of the Bluegrass State.
  1. Kentucky—Juvenile literature. [1. Kentucky]
I. Title. II. Series.
F451.3.M36 1987   976.9   87-34150
ISBN 0-516-00463-8

A quilter at Fort Boonesborough State Park

TABLE OF CONTENTS

Chapter 1   My Old Kentucky Home. 7

Chapter 2   The Land. 9

Chapter 3   The People. 21

Chapter 4   Early Settlement and Pioneer Days. 27

Chapter 5   Brother Against Brother. 39

Chapter 6   The Twentieth Century. 51

Chapter 7   Government and the Economy. 63

Chapter 8   Horses. 75

Chapter 9   Culture and Recreation. 81

Chapter 10   Touring the Bluegrass State. 91

Facts at a Glance. 109

Maps. 133

Index. 138

Chapter 1
MY OLD KENTUCKY HOME

MY OLD KENTUCKY HOME

> The sun shines bright on my old Kentucky home,
> 'Tis summer, the old folks are gay;
> The corn-top's ripe and the meadow's in the bloom,
> While the birds make music all the day.

Though Kentucky's state song, "My Old Kentucky Home," paints an unreal and sentimental picture of plantation life, there's more to the song than those first lines:

> By'n-by hard times comes a-knocking at the door,
> Then, my old Kentucky home, goodnight!
> Weep no more, my lady, Oh! weep no more today!
> We will sing one song for my old Kentucky home,
> For my old Kentucky home, far away.

These mournful words are very moving to Kentuckians who have moved away from their state. Many native-born sons and daughters can trace their family trees through several generations of Kentuckians. They're related to dozens of other Kentuckians who have always lived nearby. They don't want to leave home, and if they are forced by circumstances to move away, they can't wait to come back—at least for frequent visits.

Kentucky is a southern state, in many ways more like her Dixie neighbors than the states along her northern borders. Yet the state legislature voted to stay in the Union when war broke out between North and South.

Kentucky, like every state, is a place of contrasts. It is northern and southern, urban and rural, mountainous and flat, traditional and modern. Let's explore some of these contrasts and perhaps we'll find out why, no matter where they may go, Kentuckians never stop singing "My Old Kentucky Home."

Chapter 2
THE LAND

THE LAND

"Heaven is a Kentucky kind of place." An early preacher is supposed to have said that, and most Kentuckians think heaven will be just fine if it is as beautiful as their own state.

When the first French trappers crossed the Ohio River and the first Virginian hunters trekked over the mountains into the part of the country now known as the Commonwealth of Kentucky, they found a land thickly covered with forests. Giant trees—oak, maple, hickory, beech, poplar, sycamore, and dozens of others— had trunks of up to ten feet (three meters) in diameter. According to tales handed down through generations of Kentuckians, some families camped inside hollow trunks of sycamores until they could manage to put together a log cabin.

Nearly three-quarters of the land was virgin forest. Today, almost all of the original timber has been cut, but more than 40 percent of Kentucky is still wooded. There are woodlands in all of the state's 120 counties, and in 90 of them forestry is still an important industry. The greatest concentration of forestland is in the eastern, mountainous section.

Broadly speaking, the state can be divided into three sections: eastern, central, and western. Most geographers, however, list six regions that reflect the contrasts in geology and terrain: the Eastern Coal Field, also classified as the Appalachian Plateau, the Mountains, or the Cumberland Plateau; the Bluegrass; the Knobs; the Pennyroyal, spelled "Pennyrile" in older reference books and

A barn in the Eastern Kentucky Mountains

sometimes classified as the Mississippian Plateau; the Western
Coal Field; and the Jackson Purchase.

THE EASTERN COAL FIELD

The Eastern Coal Field occupies the portion of Kentucky
bounded on the east by Virginia, West Virginia, and a small part
of southeastern Ohio. The Pine and Cumberland mountains are
rugged and forested. The highest point in the state is here—Black
Mountain, with an elevation of 4,145 feet (1,263 meters). Even
though mining and lumbering practices destroyed much of the
original scenery, it is still a land of great natural beauty, especially
attractive to people who love the out-of-doors for hiking,
camping, and fishing. Waterfalls cascade down the slopes; high
bluffs, rocky cliffs, and natural bridges are reflected in mountain
streams and rivers. Birds and small mammals make their homes in
the forests.

As the name suggests, the economy of this region depends on
coal mining, along with marginal farming and some lumbering.
Large areas in the mountains have few, if any, inhabitants. On the
other hand, the few level areas in the mountains are very
crowded.

Louisville, located in the Bluegrass region, is the largest metropolitan area in the state.

THE BLUEGRASS

The Bluegrass is a large, roughly circular region in the north-central part of the state. The city of Lexington is in the center of the Bluegrass, and Louisville is at its western edge. The Ohio River forms its arch-shaped northern boundary.

The region has also given the state its nickname — the Bluegrass State. The lush native grass is not really blue, but it produces tiny flowers in the spring that give entire fields a blue cast. It is excellent pasture grass and forms a strong turf. Bluegrass grows superbly in the limestone soil of this region.

Most of the forests have been cleared from the region, and it is now one of the world's leading districts for crop and pasturage land. Here and there, streams run through wild glens and dells.

Large horse farms cover much of the gently rolling terrain of the Bluegrass. These gentleman farms, with their neatly fenced pastures, elegant homes, and horse barns that often appear to be even more luxurious than the houses, have the appearance of well-groomed parks stretching out to the horizon.

The Bluegrass is the state's most prosperous region, renowned for the production of beef, tobacco, and bourbon whiskey.

Louisville, the largest metropolitan area in the state, has a diversified industrial base. Its location at the Falls of the Ohio River gave it a good start as a transportation hub, and it continues to be an important crossroads, by water, rail, highway, and air.

Lexington, an industrial city and a widely respected medical center, is the world's largest burley tobacco market.

THE KNOBS

The Knobs form a small collar around the Bluegrass, separating it from the Eastern Coal Field and the Pennyroyal. The terrain is that of an irregular plain with many knob-shaped hills rising from it. Some geographers include this area with the Bluegrass.

THE PENNYROYAL

The Pennyroyal is an irregularly shaped region covering most of the south-central part of Kentucky. The name is derived from an annual plant of the mint family. The traditional native pronunciation is "pennyrile."

The Pennyroyal does not have as distinct and consistent a character of its own as do the other regions. It has been called a "place between other places," a "catch-all for what has been left out of the other five regions."

The land varies from fairly high hills and ridges in the east and southeast to gently rolling plains in the center. There are no major metropolitan areas; Bowling Green is the principal trading center.

However, many of the residents have an urban, rather than a rural, lifestyle, and quite a few small towns are primarily "bedroom communities" for people who commute to work in cities. Agriculture is somewhat diversified but consists mainly of raising livestock and tobacco.

Geologically, this is a fascinating part of the state. Scores of subterranean caves have been formed by springs and underground streams, the most famous of which, Mammoth Cave, is the center of a national park.

THE WESTERN COAL FIELD

The Western Coal Field is roughly oval in shape. The Ohio River is its northern border; the Pennyroyal loops around the rest of its perimeter. Coal mining is carried on by three methods in the hills south of the Ohio River's floodplain: underground, strip, and auger mining. The most common method is strip mining, a practice that causes problems of soil erosion and water pollution.

The larger towns of the region—Owensboro, Henderson, and Madisonville—have some manufacturing, and farms in the northern part produce corn, soybeans, and hogs.

THE JACKSON PURCHASE

A point of land pointing west at the extreme end of Kentucky, smaller than the other five regions, is known as the Jackson Purchase. Andrew Jackson, before he became president, was one of the signers of a treaty by which the Chickasaw Indians sold the land to the United States, in 1818.

Before the days of railroads and modern highways, the Jackson Purchase was quite isolated from the rest of the state. Rivers form three of its boundaries: the Mississippi on the west, the Ohio on the north, and the Cumberland and Tennessee rivers on the east.

Paducah, the only urban center in the region, has some industry and is a center of trade and transportation for the tobacco, soybeans, and livestock raised on the region's fertile farms. It is an important port on the Ohio River and became an early rail center as well. Today it also has the advantage of superhighways.

In recent years, the tourism industry has boomed around Kentucky Lake, Lake Barkley, and The Land Between the Lakes.

Swamps and lowlands near the Mississippi River are popular with birdwatchers, especially during migration seasons.

One part of the Jackson Purchase, a tiny circle barely three miles in diameter, is completely cut off from the rest of the state by a loop of the Mississippi River. The only way to reach it by road is from Tennessee.

RIVERS AND LAKES

The waterways of Kentucky have played a large role in making the state the kind of place it is. The earliest explorers from the north came into the territory by boat. Abundant water supplies create a lush environment for agriculture in the areas where the soil is thick and rich. Water power for industry is readily available. Nearly 1,000 miles (1,609 kilometers) of navigable waterways are used for commercial transportation. The major rivers in Kentucky are the Licking, Kentucky, Salt, Cumberland, Green, Tennessee, Tradewater, and Barren.

The state's streams, rivers, and lakes are also popular for recreation—boating, swimming, fishing, water skiing, and other water sports. Kentucky's state park system, one of the best in the nation, makes good use of these natural resources.

Laurel River Lake, near Corbin, is one of the many lakes in Kentucky that have been formed by the construction of river dams.

Many miles of streams and rivers within the state are ideal for boating and canoeing. Some are wide, deep, and quietly scenic; others have swift white water. There are stretches of deep forests and pleasant fields; other sections pass through deep, rugged gorges and past magnificent bluffs. Some go through wilderness areas inhabited by rare and endangered wildlife.

Several of Kentucky's largest lakes have been formed by the Tennessee Valley Authority (TVA), which constructed huge dams along the Tennessee and Cumberland rivers. Major man-made lakes are Barkley, Kentucky, Harrington, Cumberland, and Dale Hollow. Smaller, natural lakes are the result of slow erosion of the land over thousands of years.

CAVES

Millions of years ago, Kentucky was under water, part of a shallow body called the Mississippian Sea. As forces beneath the earth pushed the land upward, the sea gradually moved south toward the Gulf of Mexico. Rainwater washed away some of the newly exposed land and soaked through what was left. This

Two of Kentucky's most spectacular caverns are the onyx chamber in Mammoth Cave National Park (left) and Diamond Caverns in Park City (above).

process of erosion created sinkholes and gradually carved out a network of channels beneath the surface.

Much of the rock underlying south-central and eastern Kentucky is limestone, a substance easily eroded and even dissolved, in time, by water. Movement of underground streams carves out narrow passages, some of which eventually become broad corridors and rooms. Today there are dozens of caverns underneath the hills and farmlands of the region. Some of them are huge and world famous; many others are still unexplored.

As the rooms and corridors are formed, water slowly seeps through and dissolves the limestone ceilings of the caves. The drops of water form stalactites that grow down from the top and stalagmites that build up from the floor beneath. These formations, found only in caves, are like rock-solid icicles. In some dry spots, deposits of gypsum create other beautiful formations, some resembling flowers.

Different minerals present in the limestone give the cave formations many variations in color. Iron oxide adds deep browns, tans, yellows, and reds to the rock; manganese creates blues, greens, and purples. Endless brilliant combinations of these colors can be seen in Kentucky's caves.

At Mammoth Cave, one of the world's largest caves open to the public, huge arched ceilings create underground amphitheaters. Giant pillars remind visitors of those seen in ancient temples and medieval cathedrals. The names given to several fantastic formations suggest their similarity to other wonders of the world: Frozen Niagara, Hindu Temple, Ruins of Karnak. Boats are rowed on the subterranean waters of Mammoth Cave, which include three rivers, two lakes, and a sea.

CLIMATE

Kentucky's climate varies considerably across the 420-mile (676-kilometer) width of the state. Differences in altitude account for the fairly wide variations in temperature.

In general, the climate is temperate and healthful, with temperatures averaging 76 to 79 degrees Fahrenheit (24.4 to 26.1 degrees Celsius) in summer and 36 to 39 degrees Fahrenheit (2.8 to 3.9 degrees Celsius) in winter. It is common, however, for the thermometer to fall below 0 degrees Fahrenheit (minus 17.8 degrees Celsius) several times each year.

Average precipitation ranges from about 40 to 50 inches (102 to 127 centimeters) each year.

FLORA AND FAUNA

Kentucky's animal life includes species native to all parts of the eastern United States. At one time, bison roamed Kentucky's plains as commonly as they did in the Great Plains. The state's many small mammals include red and gray foxes, minks,

Among the flowering plants that create spectacular seasonal displays of color throughout Kentucky are azaleas (above), bluebells (far left), and mountain laurel (left).

muskrats, raccoons, opossums, squirrels, rabbits, beavers, otters, woodchucks, rodents, and—especially in the caves—bats.

More than a hundred kinds of fish swim in the lakes and streams, and nearly three hundred species of birds have been spotted. The marshlands of western Kentucky are breeding grounds for many waterfowl, and huge flocks of migratory birds pass through—some of them stopping for the winter near the mouth of the Ohio River.

Kentucky's woods and forests are particularly beautiful in spring and early summer, when rhododendrons and azaleas cover the hills with wild color. When the magnolias come into full bloom, the appearance of much of the state is almost tropical. Spring wildflowers include trillium, bloodroot, bluebell, wild ginger, violets, pinks, and lady's slipper; and in the autumn a whole new group of brilliant flowers adds a touch of beauty to that of changing leaves.

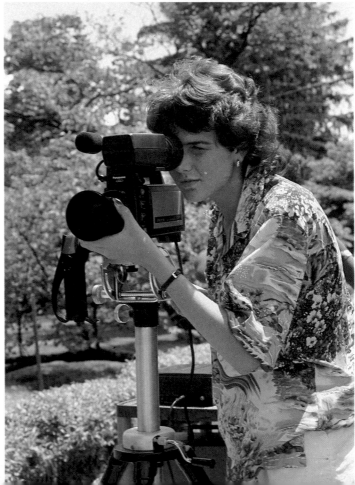

Chapter 3
THE PEOPLE

THE PEOPLE

Kentuckians have a special attachment to their home state and its heritage. They have always thought of themselves as a single ethnic group. Many of them are descended from the original settlers who migrated to Kentucky in the late 1700s and early 1800s.

Kentucky's first settlers were British subjects, colonial settlers from the states along the eastern seaboard. They were among the first Americans to venture westward, to blaze the pioneer trails and discover what was on the other side of the mountains.

Most of these earliest settlers came from Virginia and North Carolina. In 1820, three out of four of the state's residents were either English or Scottish. Language experts tell us that even today the dialect spoken in parts of the Appalachian mountains of Kentucky is similar to the English of Shakespeare's day. This indicates that in some communities there has been very little mixing with the outside world, even after all this time.

Some of the early settlers were French. In the 1850s and 1860s, quite a few German immigrants came to the cities on the Ohio River. At the end of the Civil War, one of every seven residents of Louisville was German in origin. The next wave of immigration into these cities came from Ireland.

Over the years, a number of other small groups of immigrants have arrived, but the great majority of Kentucky's people are descended from English, Scottish, Irish, and German ancestors.

Many native-born Kentuckians are descended from the original settlers who migrated to Kentucky in the late 1700s and early 1800s. They are related to dozens of other Kentuckians who have always lived nearby.

Blacks, both slave and free, have played an important part in the area's history from the beginning. In 1830, nearly a quarter of the state's population was black.

Today, a "typical" Kentucky family may live in the mountains on the same land owned by their ancestors since the early 1800s. They may be farmers on the bottomlands of the Mississippi River. They may be city people, descended from immigrants who came to Louisville for jobs in industry about a hundred years ago. Whatever part of the state they live in, they share a fierce pride in their Kentucky heritage.

Native Kentuckians also have a strong sense of regional pride, and sections of the state differ sharply in geography, culture, economics, and life-style. When Kentuckians are asked where they come from, they will invariably respond with the name of a county, rather than the larger, more general region of the state.

In general, Kentuckians have resisted moving out of the state. This picture is changing, of course. During the 1940s and 1950s, job opportunities in the cities of the Midwest, California, and Texas lured many young people away from their homes. In more recent years, more and more Americans move several times in a lifetime—not just from one home to another but across many state lines. At the same time, they are abandoning farms and country life and moving to cities. Kentuckians cannot escape these trends. In 1970, for the first time in the state's history, the United States Census Bureau discovered that more people lived in Kentucky's cities and towns than in rural areas. By 1980, nearly one-fourth of the state's population lived in its twelve largest cities.

KENTUCKY'S POPULATION TODAY

The United States census of 1980 counted 3,660,257 people living in the state of Kentucky. This is a smaller number than the population of any of the seven largest metropolitan areas of the United States (New York, Los Angeles, Chicago, Philadelphia, San Francisco, Detroit, and Boston).

Kentucky has no huge cities. Louisville, its largest, had 298,694 people in 1980, and Lexington had 204,165. Third largest was Owensboro, with only 54,450. Nevertheless, more Kentuckians now live in cities and towns (50.9 percent) than in the rural stretches of land. Less than one-fifth of the state's people are concentrated in the Appalachian regions of eastern Kentucky.

The census reported that most Kentuckians were white, native-born Americans. Blacks made up only 7 percent of the total, other minorities less than 1 percent. Fewer than 1 percent were foreign-born. Only a few thousand people spoke foreign languages at home; Spanish, German, and French were the major ones.

RELIGION

Most Kentuckians are Protestants—Baptists, Methodists, members of the Disciples of Christ (a denomination founded in this state), Presbyterians, Episcopalians, and Lutherans.

Some of the earliest explorers of the land of Kentucky were Roman Catholic priests. Catholic settlers from Maryland built a log-cabin church in Bardstown in 1798 and a cathedral in 1819. A little less than 10 percent of Kentucky's current population is Catholic.

There are very few followers of non-Christian faiths in the state.

POLITICS

Political loyalties in Kentucky today have not changed very much since the Civil War. At that time, the farmers in the eastern, mountainous part of the state were poor, eking out a living on small parcels of land. They tended to be pro-Union and Republican.

Wealthy landowners lived on the more-fertile, flatter lands of central and western Kentucky. Most were proslavery and supported the Democratic party.

These party lines have largely remained to the present time, with one exception.

In the coal-mining counties, where the United Mine Workers union gained many members and much political influence during the 1930s, the Democratic party made strong inroads in territories that had been Republican.

In Kentucky, more people vote in the Democratic primaries than in the Republican primaries; therefore, in that state, most political careers are affected by Democratic primaries. However, occasionally a Republican governor or United States senator has been elected, and Kentucky cannot be counted on as a "safe" state for the Democrats in presidential elections. Though President Carter won Kentucky in 1976, President Reagan carried the state in both 1980 and 1984.

Chapter 4

EARLY SETTLEMENT AND PIONEER DAYS

EARLY SETTLEMENT AND PIONEER DAYS

In ancient times, both Cliff Dwellers and Mound Builders occupied the bountiful land south of the Ohio River and west of the Appalachians. Archaeologists have found evidence of these early groups. Studies conducted in the 1920s identified hundreds of earth mounds, camp and village sites, cemeteries, and cliff dwellings within Kentucky's boundaries.

By the time the first European explorers discovered this beautiful region, those early inhabitants had been gone from Kentucky for at least a century. The early explorers and settlers found very few Indians living there on a permanent basis. Though some groups of Indians hunted there regularly, and intertribal battles were frequently fought in the territory, it had become a sort of no-man's-land.

Several Indian groups, however, had an interest in the land and wanted to keep the white interlopers out. The Iroquois League (the Five Nations) of New York claimed it, as did the Shawnees who lived north of the Ohio River, the Cherokees of the southern highlands, and the Chickasaws, who claimed the lands west of the Tennessee River.

These early people called the region Kentucky (spelled Kentucke until 1792). Though its English meaning is not known, the word is similar to words used by several Indian groups, each with a different interpretation. Early settlers thought it meant "dark and bloody ground"; more recently, scholars have come to believe it meant "great meadows" or "the meadowland." Another interpretation is "land of tomorrow."

EXPLORERS AND HUNTERS

Europeans made several brief expeditions into Kentucky during the late 1600s and the early 1700s. The first European known to have ventured into the Ohio Valley was French explorer René Robert Cavelier, Sieur de La Salle, who took a canoe down the Ohio River in 1669-71. In 1671, Thomas Batts and Robert Fallam were sent from Virginia by Colonel Abram Wood. Two years later, Louis Jolliet and Father Jacques Marquette saw western Kentucky during a voyage down the Mississippi River. Also in 1673, Gabriel Arthur traveled into northeastern Kentucky. Though France laid claim to the Mississippi Valley soon after this period, they did not establish any settlements in Kentucky.

It was not until the eighteenth century that a few more Europeans ventured into the territory. From the east, the Appalachian Mountains were a formidable barrier to westward expansion. Most of those who did manage to cross the mountains were hunters. Since they often spent extended periods of time hunting in Kentucky, they were called the "long hunters." Because the Indians greatly resented this trespass on some of their own favorite hunting grounds, the hunters had to be constantly on the alert if they were to stay alive.

In 1742, a trip taken by John Peter Salley from Virginia to the Ohio River rekindled English interest in the Kentucky region. Several land companies were formed in the 1740s to survey large sections of land for settlement. The Loyal Land Company sent Dr. Thomas Walker with a party of surveyors through the Cumberland Gap into Kentucky from Virginia in 1750.

In order to acquire land, the earliest Kentucky settlers had to make a claim, clear the land, build a shelter, and start a crop.

Christopher Gist visited northern Kentucky for the Ohio Land Company in 1751.

Kentucky's most famous early pioneer was Daniel Boone, who, with his brother Squire, hunted in the area. Later, he was sent by the Transylvania Land Company to blaze a trail. Boone's trail later became a famous westward route called the Wilderness Road. During the next few years, Boone and his brother wandered over much of eastern Kentucky.

EARLY SETTLEMENTS

Most of Kentucky's earliest settlers were unmarried men who came over the mountains with very few possessions besides their horses and their guns. In order to acquire land, they had to make a claim, clear the land, build a shelter, and start a crop. These men looked for parcels of land containing a good spring. The first shelters were rude little structures built of poles, only three or four feet high. They were called "improvers' cabins."

Groups of settlers followed soon after Boone's trail was opened; Boonesborough and Harrodsburg were settled during 1775.

Early pioneers lived in or near stockaded villages such as Fort Boonesborough (right). Many immigrants brought their household items to Kentucky by floating them down the Ohio River on flatboats (above).

At first, the pioneers lived in or near stockaded villages, or forts, for protection from Indian raids. These skirmishes went on for only a few years; the last battle of any significance between the new settlers and the Indians was fought at Blue Licks in 1782.

As the danger of attack lessened, the settlers laid out plans for towns. Louisville, then named Falls of the Ohio, was surveyed in 1773. The plan for Lexington was adopted in 1781. Boonesborough, Washington, and Maysville all became incorporated within a few years of each other.

When families began to immigrate into Kentucky, they brought a few household items, carried in by packhorses over the mountains or floated down the Ohio on flatboats. The first homes were simple, one-room log cabins. By the 1780s and 1790s, a few wealthy families had managed to build larger homes, some of two stories, a few made of stone or brick.

The first settlers, of course, were colonial subjects of England. Even though they were far distant from the battles of the revolutionary war, they were intensely interested in its progress.

In May 1775, Colonel Richard Henderson of the Transylvania Land Company called together what is sometimes referred to as the first Kentucky legislature.

After the American Revolution ended, Kentuckians began to think about setting up a government of their own. At this point, the territory was still technically a part of Virginia, but a movement was afoot to separate from the government on the other side of the mountains.

Starting in 1784, ten conventions were called before an agreement was reached on what form the government should take. Strong disagreements were aired: some people wanted to remain a part of Virginia; some wanted to become a part of the Spanish empire; some would have preferred complete independence; some wished to join the new Union as a state.

Finally, the last option won out, and in 1792 Kentucky became the fifteenth state, the second one after Vermont to join the original thirteen. By this time, more than 75,000 people had settled in Kentucky, and by 1800 the population of the state had exploded to 220,955.

THE NEW STATE

The constitution of the new state included a bill of rights guaranteeing freedom of religion, freedom of speech (but not false statements), freedom of the press (to publish facts and honest opinions), freedom to meet for peaceful purposes, the right to keep and bear arms, the right of trial by jury, and other rights— twenty-eight items in all. The state's government was set up like the federal government, with three branches—executive, legislative, and judicial—with separation of powers.

The constitution was very democratic for the times. No requirements of religion or property were to be imposed as a condition of voting—all white males and free black males twenty-one years of age and older were to have the right to vote.

Members of the constitutional convention disagreed on the issue of slavery. Nine of the members were ministers, and all of them wanted to prohibit ownership of slaves in Kentucky. They paid a price for taking this stand; the constitution as adopted not only permitted slavery but prohibited "ministers of religious societies" from holding public office while still serving as religious leaders. However, after 1789, no more slaves were to be brought into the state from a foreign country.

Kentucky's official name is the Commonwealth of Kentucky. Though the terms *commonwealth* and *state* were used synonymously in those days, commonwealth literally means "for the good of all."

All of the conventions had been held in Danville, but it was not selected as the site of the state capital. Lexington, then the largest city in the state, became the temporary capital, and the General Assembly, at its first session, selected Frankfort to be the permanent seat of state government.

The Mississippi River was an essential artery for the shipment of Kentucky products south to New Orleans, so the Louisiana Purchase, negotiated by President Thomas Jefferson in 1803, was greatly appreciated by Kentuckians. It brought the lands on both sides of the river into the United States.

Known as the Great Compromiser, Kentucky politician Henry Clay was an eloquent speaker and a master mediator. An important national political leader for many years, Clay worked tirelessly to find ways to bring opposing factions together.

HENRY CLAY

The new country was expanding and Kentucky politicians who favored this expansion were popular. One of these was Henry Clay, a young man who was elected to the Kentucky state legislature in 1803 and proved himself so capable that in 1806 he was sent to the United States Senate to fill out another senator's unexpired term.

Clay, an eloquent speaker, was an important political leader for many years. He was elected to the United States House of Representatives in 1811 and was immediately chosen Speaker of the House, a position he held for six terms.

Tensions had been building again between Britain and the United States. Clay was a leader of a group of westerners who were called war hawks because they favored war with Britain. His constituents were solidly behind him on this issue, and as soon as the War of 1812 began, thousands of Kentuckians were ready to participate in the fighting.

Clay often worked tirelessly to find ways to bring opposing factions together. For this reason, he is known in American history as the Great Compromiser.

One of the most famous incidents in which Clay exerted strong influence is known as the Missouri Compromise of 1820, when the factions on both sides of the slavery issue were persuaded to admit Missouri as a slave state and Maine as a free state. His role in formulating the Compromise of 1850 (the Great Compromise), which helped delay the Civil War for ten years, further enhanced his reputation.

Henry Clay ran for the presidency of the United States three times, but never won. His reaction to his several defeats was, "I had rather be right than be president." In 1824, he was one of four candidates. Since none of the four received a majority of the votes, the United States House of Representatives had to choose from among the top three. Clay, who was last, threw his support behind John Quincy Adams, who became president and selected Clay to be his secretary of state.

KENTUCKY GROWS AND PROSPERS

Most Kentuckians in the early 1800s were farmers. The use of steamboats on the Ohio and Mississippi rivers, which started in 1811, was an important aid in the shipment of agricultural products. In 1830, a canal was completed on the Louisville side of the Falls of the Ohio; this made two-way steamboat traffic possible between Pittsburgh and New Orleans. The first railroad service in the state was established in 1835. Several roads were constructed, and between them the roads and railroads furnished stiff competition to the riverboats and increased greatly the ease of transporting goods.

By 1850, Louisville had a population of nearly 45,000 and Lexington (above) was a rapidly growing metropolis.

The War of 1812 gave an impetus to the production of iron and the manufacture of textiles in the state, and commercial coal mining began to be economically important.

By 1850, the population of Kentucky was four times as great as it had been at the turn of the century, and the state was a leader in the production of distilled liquors, livestock, tobacco, corn, hemp, and flax, as well as coal and iron.

EDUCATION

Kentucky's first schools were founded by churches and church-related groups. Transylvania Seminary, opened near Danville in 1785, moved to Lexington in 1788. In 1798, as Transylvania Academy, it joined with Presbyterian Kentucky Academy to become Transylvania University. This was one of the earliest universities in the nation, and claims to be the first college chartered west of the Alleghenies.

During the Kentucky Revival era, people flocked to religious camp meetings to hear the leading evangelistic preachers of the day.

In the 1820s and 1830s, several colleges were founded by churches—Methodist, Catholic, Presbyterian, Baptist, and Disciples of Christ. The University of Louisville, whose roots go back to 1837, claims to be the oldest city university in the United States.

RELIGION

One of the most interesting and unusual historical movements in Kentucky during this period was the Kentucky Revival. It started with a series of religious camp meetings held toward the end of the 1790s and continued until the Civil War. People flocked to these meetings from many miles around, bringing with them enough food and camping supplies to last for a week.

Huge crowds of ten to fifteen thousand people would come to hear the leading evangelistic preachers of the day, whose sermons were highly emotional in their appeal. Hundreds of people were converted during the services, and church membership rolls

One of Kentucky's early Catholic churches was St. Joseph's Cathedral (left), built in Bardstown in 1819. The Pleasant Hill village founded by the Shakers has been restored to its appearance in 1830 (above).

increased tremendously. The leading denominations involved in the camp meetings were the Presbyterians and Methodists. Differences of opinion as to doctrine led to a split in the Presbyterian Church and the founding of the Christian Church, the only major Protestant denomination whose roots are purely American.

An interesting small sect known as the Shakers founded two communities in Kentucky during this period. All members of the group lived and ate in large, dormitory-type buildings. All property was owned by the group, and everyone obeyed the rules of the society, which included a ban on marriage and childbearing. There are very few Shakers today, but the village they established at Pleasant Hill, south of Lexington, has been restored to its appearance of 1830 and is open to the public.

The Catholic Church was established in Kentucky during the late 1700s. One of the early Catholic churches was founded in Bardstown around 1798, and St. Joseph's Cathedral was built there in 1819.

Chapter 5
BROTHER AGAINST BROTHER

BROTHER AGAINST BROTHER

Slavery was legal in Kentucky from the beginning, even though an outspoken minority of the delegates to the constitutional convention had opposed it.

By the 1830s, opposition to slavery had increased considerably in the state. However, most people favored a gradual approach to ending the practice and disagreed with the more-radical antislavery advocates who were known as abolitionists. Though a large proportion of Kentucky farmers were slaveholders, the number of slaves each household had was quite small. Kentucky's land was not suited for the raising of sugarcane or cotton on large plantations needing many field hands.

But even though their pro-slavery feelings were not as strongly emotional as in much of the South, Kentuckians had a strong kinship with and loyalty to the rest of the slaveholding southern states. After all, most Kentucky families were directly descended from pioneers from Virginia, the Carolinas, and Tennessee.

The abolitionist movement in the northern states was gathering steam. Abolitionists believed that slavery was absolutely evil, and that it should be stopped instantly by any means that could be found. Some of them even made a practice of coming into Kentucky to meet secretly with slaves and try to influence them to make a break for freedom in the North.

More-moderate slaveholders, such as Henry Clay, wanted to see slavery ended but were concerned about possible problems if

By the 1830s, opposition to slavery had taken many forms in Kentucky. Of those who wanted the practice ended gradually, some urged freed blacks to sail to the African colony of Liberia on ships such as the *Azor* (left). Cassius M. Clay (above) and other abolitionists demanded an immediate end to slavery by any means that could be found.

slaves were set free with no means of earning a living. A group of these moderates organized the American Colonization Society in 1816. The society set up a colony in Africa, called Liberia, where freed blacks could organize a country of their own.

The abolitionist Liberty party was the first political party in the United States to give most of its attention to the slavery question. Kentuckian James G. Birney, a former slaveholder, was the party's presidential nominee in 1840 and again in 1844. In 1848, the Liberty party united with other groups to form the Free Soil party.

A Kentucky native named Cassius M. Clay published *The True American*, an emancipationist newspaper in Lexington, for a short time in 1845. Attacks by angry crowds of pro-slavery Kentuckians soon forced Clay to move his publication to Cincinnati, Ohio.

The slavery issue caused three major Protestant denominations—the Methodists, Presbyterians, and Baptists—to split into northern and southern branches, and the split remained for many decades after the close of the Civil War.

By the 1850s, when war between North and South began to seem inevitable, most Kentuckians wanted to remain neutral. The state was right in the center of the nation's settled states. Its citizens believed they could be of great service to their country by providing refuge to both sides and acting as peacemakers.

President Abraham Lincoln had indicated in the beginning that he would not interfere with slavery in those states in which it was legal. This stand convinced many Kentuckians that they might be able to keep their slaves and still remain loyal to the Union. The state legislature adopted an official resolution in May 1861 declaring that the state would take no part in the war on either side and would "occupy the position of strict neutrality." But circumstances soon forced a choosing of sides. By September, a new legislature declared in favor of the Union.

The border state of Kentucky was caught in the middle. It tried to remain friendly to both the North and the South, but soon found that it was neither respected nor protected by either side.

THE WAR BETWEEN THE STATES

Representatives of six southern states met at Montgomery, Alabama, in 1861. They decided that the time had come to secede from the United States and form a separate government, the Confederate States of America. This step made war unavoidable.

Symbolic of the conflicting loyalties in Kentucky is the fact that both presidents—Abraham Lincoln of the Union, and Jefferson Davis of the Confederacy—were born in this state. Tens of thousands of Kentuckians fought on both sides of the Civil War. And in family after family, relatives fought against relatives.

In November 1861, Kentucky secessionists claiming to represent sixty-five counties organized their own state government. The group was admitted to the Confederacy as the twelfth Confederate state. Kentucky had a star in both flags—Confederate and Union.

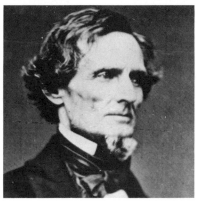

Photographer Mathew Brady's record of the Civil War includes photographs of both Kentucky-born presidents—Abraham Lincoln of the Union (top, in the center) and Jefferson Davis of the Confederacy (above)—as well as hundreds of others, including Union (left) and Confederate soldiers.

On January 1, 1863, President Lincoln issued his Emancipation Proclamation, freeing all slaves held by persons residing in "States or parts of States wherein the people thereof, respectively, are . . . in rebellion against the United States." All the border states except Kentucky and Delaware proceeded to abolish slavery by state law. In those two states, slaveholding remained legal until the adoption of the Thirteenth Amendment in 1865.

Because of Lincoln's earlier statements, Kentuckians felt betrayed by the Emancipation Proclamation. Then came further

The repeal of the Fugitive Slave Law and the drafting of black troops into the Union army were only two of the events that helped turn public opinion in the border state of Kentucky more and more away from the Union.

blows: the drafting into the Union army of black troops and the repeal of the Fugitive Slave Law, which had protected the right of a slaveholder to recover a runaway slave.

Thus, as the war went on, public opinion in Kentucky turned more and more away from the Union. Nevertheless, thousands of Kentuckians mourned with their northern neighbors when Lincoln was assassinated. Many believed that if he had lived, the state would not have been treated so harshly during the postwar period. Today, Kentucky honors Abraham Lincoln as a native son and preserves the landmarks associated with his birth and boyhood.

AFTERMATH OF THE WAR

After the war, the Union military forces treated Kentucky as a defeated, occupied enemy because so many of its citizens were known to be sympathetic to the Confederacy. Lincoln had placed the state under martial law, and this order remained in force until October 1865. Thus, anti-Union sentiment continued to grow even after the war ended. Former Confederates soon gained political power, and dominated the Democratic party in the state until 1895.

Kentucky suffered very heavy losses among its soldiers. In

addition, the state was in economic shambles as a result of guerilla raids on crops and livestock, destruction of transportation systems, and the loss of millions of dollars' worth of slaves.

NEW POSITION OF BLACKS

With the freeing of slaves at the end of the Civil War, blacks found new problems to replace the hardships they had endured as slaves. Former slaves had difficulty finding employment in the cities and towns. Thousands of them were forced to continue working at the same kinds of jobs they had had before—field work on farms or plantations and domestic work in the homes of wealthy white families.

Since nearly twenty-five thousand black soldiers from Kentucky had fought for the Union, they were impatient to achieve freedom and the other rights that should go along with freedom. The Thirteenth Amendment, ratified on December 6, 1865, abolished slavery. The Fourteenth, officially giving citizenship to former slaves, took two and a half years to be ratified. And the Fifteenth, declaring that the right to vote could not be denied to anyone because of "race, color, or previous conditions of servitude," did not become official until 1870.

Meanwhile, in 1866, Kentucky's legislature had passed an act giving civil rights to blacks, but it had little real meaning. Less than 17 percent of the population were blacks, and because of the prior restraints of slavery, most were without property or much education. Nevertheless, they were aware of their rights as Americans and worked together to achieve them.

The Ku Klux Klan (KKK), organized in 1866 by a group of former Confederate soldiers, was determined to prevent blacks from exercising those rights. Klansmen, outfitted in white robes and hoods, embarked on a five-year reign of terror during which they attacked, threatened, and murdered blacks and those whites who supported civil rights for blacks.

During that period, blacks were not allowed to testify in the state courts in any cases involving whites. If a white person committed a crime against a black person, it could be proved only if there were white witnesses willing to testify.

When cases were brought to the federal courts, however, decisions were handed down that helped change the worst of the inequalities. Three important civil-rights laws were eventually passed in the state during the postwar period—an equalization law for education, a law granting equality in testimony, and an act to control lawlessness.

Despite the problems that confronted them, many blacks managed to build homes, raise families, and begin a new life.

EDUCATION

The Civil War had nearly destroyed all public education in Kentucky. Various measures were taken in the 1870s to change the situation, and a slow process of improvement began. After 1908, all of the larger cities and many of the smaller ones had public high schools. Most higher education was furnished by private institutions.

Before the war, few educational opportunities had been furnished for blacks. In 1866, however, the Kentucky legislature passed a law to provide some funding for black schools. School segregation was public policy in Kentucky from the beginning, and funds allotted for blacks were far from adequate. Some districts had less than $50 a year to support a school. Three schools were set up to train black teachers, but they did not survive long.

World-famous Berea College, founded before the Civil War, was chartered in 1866. Its philosophy was that everyone should have an opportunity to get a college education, regardless of race, religion, or financial resources. Blacks were admitted and continued to be educated at Berea until state law prohibited integrated education in 1904.

SEGREGATION

In 1895, Homer Plessy, a black man from Louisiana, took a seat in the section of a train reserved for whites only. He was arrested, and his case went all the way to the United States Supreme Court. In 1896, the Supreme Court decided that the Louisiana law dictating "separate but equal" facilities for whites and blacks was constitutional. This decision made it legal for any state to enforce the separation of races in any and all public facilities.

The pattern of segregation set by the Plessy decision was to remain as a rigid way of life in the South for the next sixty years. Blacks and whites were forbidden to eat together in public places or sit together on buses and trains until another black—Rosa Parks of Montgomery, Alabama—took a seat in the "white" section of a bus, refused to move, and set in motion the civil-rights movement of the 1960s.

Finally, more than one hundred years after blacks were freed from slavery, flagrant discrimination ceased to be condoned by United States law.

During the Civil War, the West Virginia Hatfield family (above) and the Kentucky McCoy family began a feud that lasted for more than thirty years.

HATFIELDS AND McCOYS

Ill feelings over the Civil War did not die easily. Many friends and neighbors found it hard to forgive one another for differing loyalties during the war.

For more than thirty years after peace was declared, two mountain families—the Hatfields of Mingo County, West Virginia, and the McCoys, of Pike County, Kentucky—were still battling over old hurts. Their disagreements led to the most famous, or infamous, feud in American history.

Most of the Hatfields had supported the Confederates; most McCoys were loyal to the North. One McCoy, a Union leader, was killed in 1863, and his body was found near the Hatfield home. Accusations of various crimes and wrongdoings were hurled back and forth for years, and a series of revenge killings took place. At least twenty people—some estimates are as high as one hundred—died as a direct result of the bad feelings.

This illustration, based on a photo, shows an auction sale of tobacco in Louisville, which by 1900 was the world's largest tobacco market.

THE POSTWAR ECONOMY

A few years after the Civil War ended, the problems of the war and postwar period faded into the background. Kentucky, along with the rest of the country, was undergoing many changes in industry, agriculture, and commerce.

Louisville merchants moved aggressively to reestablish the markets in the South that had been so important to them before the war. They sent out salesmen, or "drummers," to drum up business and extended credit to southern storekeepers.

Farming was still the most important occupation for Kentuckians, but city population was increasing more rapidly than rural population. Tobacco was the most important farm crop; three times as much tobacco was grown in 1900 as in 1870, and Louisville was the world's largest tobacco market. Other important farm products were livestock, hay, wheat, corn, dairy products, and hemp.

Coal mining was becoming more and more important in Kentucky, and the increase in the number of rail lines on which coal could be shipped was a great help to this industry. By 1900, Kentucky was third in the nation in coal production.

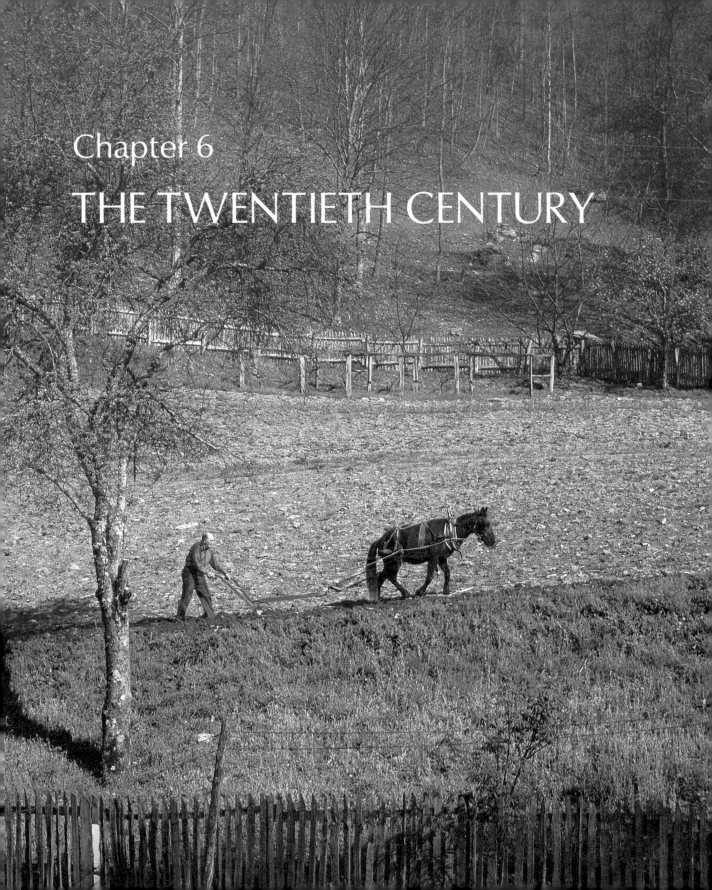

Chapter 6

THE TWENTIETH CENTURY

THE TWENTIETH CENTURY

Four out of five Kentuckians lived on farms at the beginning of the 1900s. Many of these farms were small and the families who lived on them had very little cash.

A RURAL WAY OF LIFE

Farm families raised much of their own food—vegetables, grain, chickens, and a hog or two. Almost every young boy grew up knowing how to catch fish and shoot small game; these foods didn't cost money. The few items that required cash could usually be obtained through barter.

The women of the households made most of the clothing needed by family members. By that time, they may have given up spinning and weaving their own cloth, and those who could afford them used modern sewing machines. But most items of apparel were sewn at home.

Baseball was popular throughout the state. Louisville's major-league baseball team was a member of the American Association. The manufacture of baseball bats became an important Louisville industry at about that time, and Louisville Slugger bats, used throughout the baseball world, were made there until recently.

Cars were still rare in this part of the country. People got around by foot, on muleback, or by horsedrawn wagons or buggies. By then, the state had quite a network of railroads, and trains provided transportation for long trips.

At the beginning of the 1900s, the modern city of Louisville could boast that it had electric lights, electric streetcars, telephones, movie theaters, and even a few automobiles.

Louisville was rapidly becoming a modern city. Electric lights, electric streetcars, telephones, and even a few automobiles were in use. Moving pictures were shown in Louisville even before 1900, but it would be a few more years before they became popular.

In the hills and valleys of rural Kentucky, however, everyday life had not changed much for forty years or so. Not all rural children went to school, and those who did received only a few months of schooling each year. Few went beyond the sixth grade.

In 1908 and 1909, the state voters sent representatives to Frankfort who became known as the "Educational Legislature." They increased funds for the support of public schools and introduced changes that resulted in more-equal educational opportunities throughout the state. Schools were required to be in session for at least six months of each year, and a free public high school was to be organized in each county.

THE TOBACCO WAR

Tobacco farmers had a difficult time during the early part of the century. The so-called Tobacco War was a period of lawlessness that lasted from 1904 to 1909. The price of tobacco had fallen to a very low point, and some of the farmers wanted to organize into groups that would pool their crops and store them for a while, holding out for higher prices.

Quite a few farmers felt they could not afford to hold out, and refused to join the pools. Those who were in the pools would gather at night and vandalize the farms of those who had not joined. They were called Night Riders. They rode about the countryside destroying newly planted beds and crops growing in the fields, and setting fire to tobacco barns. Hundreds of thousands of dollars' worth of property was destroyed. The lawlessness ended only after the new Republican governor, Augustus E. Willson, called out the state militia and prosecuted Night Riders.

A NEW INDUSTRY

When rich seams of bituminous coal were discovered in eastern Kentucky in 1911, northern corporations built railroads into the area and started mine operations.

Thousands of giant trees were stripped from entire hillsides as these enterprises began. The way had to be cleared for the railroads, and wood was needed for the railroad ties and for construction. So down went chestnuts, hickories, buckeyes, maples, and huge tulip poplars and oak trees. The topsoil, robbed of the tree roots that had held it in place, washed into streams and created mudslides.

WORLD WAR I

About eighty thousand Kentuckians were members of the armed forces of the United States during World War I. Four military training camps were located within the state.

The war created boom times for the new mines, as huge amounts of coal were needed to provide fuel for the steel mills and other northern factories. Fortunes were made and hundreds of Kentucky farmers were drawn out of the hills to work in the mines, where they could earn more cash in a month than farming had brought them in a year.

COMPANY TOWNS

The mining companies built towns overnight to house the workers. Attractive when new, they deteriorated when hard times hit. Streets were unpaved and full of mudholes; houses were little more than rickety shacks; there was electricity, but no indoor plumbing; wells and streams were polluted.

The miners needed places to buy food and a few other necessities, so the companies set up stores. Prices were high, but the miners had no place else to go. They used "scrip"—paper money or brass tokens issued to them by their employers—to buy on credit at a company store. As a result, they almost never had any cash. Their wages went back to the company for rent, food, fuel, and electricity as fast as they were earned.

A popular song called "Sixteen Tons," written by Merle Travis, includes the following lyrics:

> Sixteen tons and what do you get?
> You get another day older and deeper in debt.
> Saint Peter, don't you call me 'cause I can't go,
> I owe my soul to the company store.

Travis's father, a Kentucky coal miner who was required to dig sixteen tons of coal a day for his wages, rarely had anything to show for his efforts except a debt to the company store.

Even though mine-safety regulations have reduced the death rate from mine accidents by 85 percent since the early 1900s, today's underground coal miners still must work in dark, confined spaces.

DARK AS A DUNGEON

Though jobs in the mines were eagerly sought, the work was unbelievably hard. Working conditions were uncomfortable, difficult, and dangerous. There was the constant danger of a cave-in or an explosion. Many miners were killed or disabled, and before long all of them realized that anyone who continued to work in the mines for many years was almost certain, eventually, to become ill with an incurable lung disease.

"Dark as a Dungeon," another song written by Merle Travis, describes the terrible working conditions in the mines:

> Come all you young fellows so young and so fine,
> Seek not your fortune in the dark dreary mine.
> It will form like a habit and seep in your soul
> Till the stream of your blood is as black as the coal.
> It's dark as a dungeon, and damp as the dew;
> The dangers are many, and the pleasures are few,
> Where the rain never falls and the sun never shines—
> It's dark as a dungeon, way down in the mines.

With the end of World War I, the coal-mining boom ended. During the 1920s, many miners lost their jobs; those who were left were forced to take cuts in pay. And by this time, nearly everyone in the mining counties was totally dependent on the coal industry for an income. Families were no longer able to get by on the products of their small farms—in fact, many of them had sold their land for pitifully small amounts.

Efforts to organize the workers into labor unions met with strong and violent opposition from the mine operators. Strikes and battles between strikers and strikebreakers resulted. There was so much lawlessness in one southeastern Kentucky county that it became known as "Bloody Harlan County."

DEPRESSION

As the nation slid into the Great Depression of the 1930s, conditions in Kentucky became even worse.

President Franklin D. Roosevelt's economic reforms brought some relief. Many important projects conducted by the Works Progress Administration (WPA) and Public Works Administration (PWA) created jobs for the state's residents. Among other projects, modern school buildings were constructed in all sections of the state, and the PWA adult-education program helped to lower the illiteracy rate.

As the depression grew more and more serious, workers all over the country began to join labor unions in increasing numbers. Kentucky miners were a part of this movement. Congress passed the Wagner Labor Relations Act, which guaranteed the right of workers to join unions and bargain collectively with their employers. In September 1938, an agreement signed between the United Mine Workers of America and the coal-mine operators led to substantial improvements in wages and working conditions.

Since 1936, the federal government's gold reserves have been kept at Fort Knox in this heavily guarded granite, steel, and concrete building.

Even during the worst years of the depression, new inventions and developments were at work that would, before long, make far-reaching changes in the lives of rural people. Radio was bringing news of the outside into the most remote areas of the country. Improved highways made it easier for residents of rural areas to go to the city and for city-made products to be brought to the country. Automobiles were becoming common, and along with them came service stations, garages, and tourist camps.

Air service, for both passengers and freight, linked Louisville with Cincinnati and Indianapolis in the mid-1920s, and ten thousand people flocked to greet Charles Lindbergh when he flew his *Spirit of St. Louis* into Bowman Field in 1928.

In 1936, an army post thirty-five miles south of Louisville became the most valuable piece of property in the world. That was the year the United States Treasury Department deposited the federal government's gold reserves at Fort Knox. Gold—billions of dollars' worth—is kept there in a heavily guarded, two-story, granite, steel, and concrete building.

Albert B. "Happy" Chandler was appointed baseball commissioner in 1946.

GOVERNOR "HAPPY" CHANDLER

In 1935, Albert B. "Happy" Chandler was elected governor of Kentucky. He managed to repeal the sales tax, and even though both the tobacco and liquor industries were very important to Kentucky's economy, Chandler was able to put through new taxes on these products. As a result, the poorer people in the state no longer had to pay sales taxes on items such as food and clothing; the industries making large profits made up the difference.

Toward the end of his term as governor, Chandler was appointed to fill a vacancy in the United States Senate, and later was appointed baseball commissioner. In 1955, he was elected governor of Kentucky for another term.

ALBEN W. BARKLEY

Another national political leader from Kentucky during this period was Alben W. Barkley. The son of a poor tenant farmer, Barkley worked his way through college and law school and went on to national prominence. Elected to the United States House of Representatives in 1912, he served seven consecutive terms. He was elected to the Senate in 1926, and held the post of majority leader from 1937 to 1947.

President Harry S. Truman selected Barkley to be his running mate in 1948, and Barkley became vice-president of the United States. He was very popular and was known far and wide by the affectionate nickname "the Veep." After completing his term as vice-president, Barkley again ran for the Senate in 1954, was elected, and held office until his death less than two years later.

WORLD WAR II AND THE POSTWAR BOOM

World War II and the industrial boom times that followed it ended forever the isolation of many Kentucky farm families.

Thousands of men registered with the Selective Service, then either volunteered or were drafted into the army, navy, or other services. Women took on new roles, either joining one of the newly organized military services for women—the women Marines, WAAC, WAVE, or WAAF—or going into the factories to produce planes, tanks, and other goods needed for the war effort.

When the conflict ended, factories in northern cities continued to recruit large numbers of workers from Kentucky and other southern states. They placed prominent ads in newspapers, offering relatively high wages to convince thousands of southerners to migrate northward.

The war had brought another boom period to the coal industry because of increased need for fuel to run the busy factories. Then, in the 1950s, the mining companies started a price war, cut back on expensive safety measures, and slashed wages. Even these drastic steps were not enough to save many of the corporations from bankruptcy. One after another, mining towns were deserted and buildings were boarded up and left to fall into ruin.

TODAY

The state's population has continued to grow, but at a much slower pace than during earlier periods and more slowly than the United States as a whole. Urban counties are gaining in numbers but rural ones are losing as young people move to Louisville, Cincinnati, Detroit, Chicago, and other metropolitan centers. By 1970, for the first time in the state's history, more Kentuckians were living in cities and towns than on farms and in rural villages.

The development of the interstate highway system has made it easier for the people of Kentucky to travel both within and outside the state. Many Kentuckians commute some distance to jobs in Kentucky and other states; they also travel regularly to Cincinnati, Ohio; Evansville, Indiana; and Nashville, Tennessee for shopping and entertainment. The Cincinnati Reds baseball team is as popular south of the Ohio River as it is at home.

Louisville, the only city in the state with a large industrial base, is almost more midwestern in flavor than southern. Lexington is a major service and trade center for eastern Kentucky. Paducah, Bowling Green, and Owensboro are centers of both industry and service businesses.

One of the major problems facing Kentucky is education. Its rank among the states in the average level of education is quite low. Though state support for schools is good, funding at the local level is not adequate.

CIVIL RIGHTS

In Kentucky, the Civil Rights Movement of the 1960s improved the status of blacks without causing as many problems or as much violence as experienced in some other states. Because Kentucky

Built as part of a downtown Louisville beautification and redevelopment program, the glass-enclosed Louisville Galleria on the Fourth Avenue Mall draws shoppers from the city as well as visitors from other parts of the state and neighboring states.

has a smaller percentage of black residents than that of most southern states, discrimination was not quite so deeply rooted.

In 1964, the Kentucky General Assembly was considering the passage of an anti-discrimination law. Progress was slow, however, and the Reverend Martin Luther King, Jr. led a civil-rights march in Frankfort. Some of the marchers took part in a five-day hunger strike. They remained in the gallery of the house of representatives until it adjourned, still without action on the bill. At the end of the session, Governor Edward Breathitt met with hunger strikers and promised to support further efforts to pass a bill to outlaw discrimination in public places. During the next session of the Kentucky legislature, in 1966, a strong civil-rights act was passed by a large majority.

Kentucky was the first southern state to enact such a law. It made discrimination in public accommodations illegal, and prohibited discriminatory hiring practices by employers of more than eight people. In 1968, before the United States Congress acted on a similar measure, the state passed an open-housing law.

Chapter 7

GOVERNMENT AND THE ECONOMY

GOVERNMENT AND THE ECONOMY

Counties in Kentucky are far more important units of government than they are in many other states. Some observers say that real political power is held at the county level.

KENTUCKY COUNTIES

There are 120 counties in the commonwealth; more than in any other state except Texas and Georgia. County government was much more powerful during the first half of the nineteenth century than it is today. County officers held legislative, executive, and judicial power in their hands—a serious violation of the American principle of separation of the three branches of government. County courts had the power to regulate certain businesses, appoint the officials who enforced the law, supervise the collection of taxes, and judge the merits of local cases.

It was a very undemocratic situation. The courts were made up of justices of the peace, who were not elected. They were empowered to fill their own vacancies. The procedure was for the retiring justice to submit to the governor two possible candidates for each vacancy. The governor nearly always appointed one of the suggested candidates. Besides selecting new members of their own body, the justices had the authority to appoint all county officers: sheriffs, constables, surveyors, coroners, inspectors, county clerks, and others.

The governor's mansion, Frankfort

Justices had a great amount of control over any election. Voting was done openly, by a show of hands or a voice vote, so it was easy to use bribes and threats to convince the voters to go along with what the justices wanted.

The original intent was that county seats should be located within an easy day's journey for all its residents. Therefore, each county had to be fairly small, because roads were poor or nonexistent and, in some parts of the state, the terrain was rough and hilly. Whenever a group of people got together and decided that it was inconvenient to travel to the existing county seat, they petitioned the legislature to cut their county into even smaller pieces.

Kentucky had 9 counties when it became a state, nearly 60 by the time of the War of 1812, and 110 when the Civil War began. Ten have been created since.

County courts met once a month, and hundreds of people traveled to the county seat when court was in session. They came to record deeds, process wills, apply for licenses or franchises, and bring various petitions before the court. Since nearly every citizen had to deal with the county court in one way or another, court days also became the time when people gathered to trade their crops and livestock, socialize, and generally have a good time.

Many of the excesses and undemocratic practices of those early days were eliminated when Kentucky's constitution was rewritten in 1850. But even today, the county is a powerful unit of government in this state.

THE FOURTH CONSTITUTION

The Commonwealth of Kentucky has had four constitutions during its nearly two hundred years of statehood. The most recent, and the one under which the government now operates, dates from 1891.

Between 1850 and 1892, when the third and fourth constitutions went into effect, the population of Kentucky doubled. Many new towns were formed, and small towns became cities. The Industrial Revolution was in full swing, and giant corporations had been formed that were not contributing any taxes to the state. A system of public roads was needed, as were increased facilities for public education. A serious defect in the 1850 constitution was the lack of a provision for changes by amendment.

These conditions, and other changed circumstances brought about by the Civil War, made the writing of a new constitution imperative.

Many of the provisions of the 1891 constitution are similar to constitutions of other states and of the United States. There is a Bill of Rights, as there had been in each of the three previous constitutions. This one, however, has an added section prohibiting slavery.

There are three separate and equal branches, just as there are in the federal government—legislative, executive, and judicial.

The legislative branch consists of a one-hundred-member house of representatives and a thirty-eight-member senate.

The governor, chief executive officer of the executive branch, is elected for a four-year term and is not eligible for reelection until after sitting out one term. In 1983, Kentucky elected its first woman governor, Martha Layne Collins.

All members of Kentucky's judicial branch are elected by popular vote. The supreme court, the highest court of the state, consists of a chief justice and six associate justices. The next-highest court is the court of appeals, with fourteen judges. The judges of both courts are elected to eight-year terms.

All properly registered citizens of the state who are eighteen years of age or over may vote. Kentucky was the second state to set the voting age at eighteen.

The constitution also provided for voting by secret ballot, a new idea at that time. In 1888, Louisville became the first American city to use the so-called Australian (secret) ballot.

EDUCATION

Before the Civil War, Kentucky had been a leader in education. Since then, because of poverty and lack of adequate support at the local level, it has not kept pace with most other states. Nevertheless, the state does have some distinguished educational institutions.

One section of the 1891 constitution stated: "The General Assembly shall, by appropriate legislation, provide for an efficient system of common schools throughout the state." It also provided for the maintenance of separate schools for whites and blacks. In

Peaceful desegregation of Louisville schools took place in the mid-1950s.

1904, the Day Law was passed, which prohibited the integration of races in all schools, even private ones.

In 1954, the United States Supreme Court declared that compulsory separation of races in public schools was unconstitutional. Shortly after that, the Kentucky Court of Appeals also declared the Day Law unconstitutional, and Louisville became the first large southern city to admit blacks to previously all-white schools. The transition to integrated education in Kentucky has not always been completely peaceful, but it has been successful.

There are twenty-eight colleges and universities in the state. Oldest is Transylvania University in Lexington, chartered in 1780. The largest are the University of Kentucky, University of Louisville, Eastern Kentucky University, and Western Kentucky University. One of the best known is Berea College in Berea, which offers students tuition-free work-study programs.

All Berea students are required to work at least ten hours a week for the college. In return for their work, they pay no tuition. Many visitors come to see what Berea is like. Among its

Kentucky's oldest college is Transylvania (above);
the largest is the University of Kentucky (right).

attractions for outsiders is the nationally famous Boone Tavern
Hotel and dining room, run by students. Tourists are also
impressed by the artistic handcrafted products offered for sale on
campus. Along with history, science, and the humanities, Berea
students learn an appreciation of Appalachian culture and crafts.
They create pottery, furniture, and handwoven articles, the sales
of which help pay the college bills.

Kentucky also has an excellent and wide-ranging system of
community colleges and vocational-technical schools and
education centers.

TRANSPORTATION AND COMMUNICATION

Kentucky's geographic location—right in the center of the
eastern United States—makes it a hub of distribution for
manufactured goods and raw materials throughout the eastern
United States.

Modern highways have done a great deal to bring people from
different areas together. The days are gone forever when it took
most Kentuckians half a day to get to their own county seat.
Today the state has some 69,439 miles (111,751 kilometers) of

Kentucky has nearly 70,000 miles of federal, state, and local roads. This scenic drive leads to Mammoth Cave.

federal, state, and local roads. More than 1,500 of these roads are limited-access highways (interstate routes and state parkways). Interstates 65 and 75 are main arteries running north and south. I-65 serves Louisville and Bowling Green; I-75 goes through Covington and Lexington. I-64 runs east and west between Louisville and Huntington, West Virginia, and passes through Lexington.

Kentucky's more than 1,000 miles (1,609 kilometers) of commercially navigable waterways provide water routes for the transportation of goods from inland cities to the Gulf of Mexico and the oceans.

Nineteen carriers provide rail transportation. There are commercial airports at six Kentucky cities, and three other areas are served by nearby airports in bordering states.

In the field of communication, Kentucky has 176 radio stations and 164 newspapers, 16 of which are dailies. The leading newspapers in the state are the *Louisville Courier-Journal* and the *Lexington Herald-Leader*. Three magazines published locally are *Rural Kentuckian*, with the largest circulation; *Bluegrass Magazine*; and *Back Home in Kentucky*.

KET is Kentucky's educational television network. The station can be seen throughout the state, as well as in parts of five bordering states. Programming consists of high-school and college courses for credit; general subject matter for schools; and public affairs, cultural, and children's programs.

ECONOMY

Kentucky's unemployment rate in the 1980s was a little higher than the national average, and a greater percentage of Kentuckians were living below the poverty level than in most other states. Personal income, on the average, was only about 80 percent as high as the country as a whole.

The most prosperous part of the state is the Bluegrass. The largest cities and the most industry are located there, as well as the richest farms. Horses and horse farms, of course, have given the Bluegrass its unique character.

Today, manufacturing, government, and service industries produce the largest percentage of Kentucky's gross income, though farming and mining remain important to the economy.

FARMING

As more and more Americans are becoming aware of the serious health hazards associated with smoking, tobacco is gradually losing its economic importance in Kentucky. Fifty years ago, nearly half the residents of Kentucky were farmers; between one-third and one-half of their annual cash income came from the production and sale of tobacco. By 1984, less than 1 percent of the total personal income earned in Kentucky was derived from tobacco farming.

Raising tobacco is backbreaking, painful work, especially during harvest time, as much of the labor must be done by hand. After the stalks have been cut, they are attached to sticks and left in the field to wilt (above). The tobacco is then hung in ventilated barns to cure for several weeks (left) before being taken to auction.

Among the other crops grown in Kentucky are corn, hay, soybeans, wheat, barley, and rye.

Farmers who have managed to stay in agriculture have seen many changes during the last few decades. Farm machinery has made it possible for larger parcels of land to be cultivated with less manpower. The quality of agricultural education has improved. Several factors have brought farmers out of their former isolation: better highways, increased communication by radio and television, and the consolidation of rural schools.

COAL MINING

The story of coal mining in Kentucky changes with each decade, as the nationwide demand for coal rises and falls. It is an industry that seesaws between "boom" and "bust." In some years, the price

71

Though today's federal laws require strip-mine owners to reclaim the land destroyed by surface mining, most of the land lost before 1978 has not been reclaimed.

of coal is high, new mines are opened, and jobs are easy to find. In other years, the price of coal drops, and the miners are thrown out of work and plunged overnight into poverty.

When new operators came along after the bust of the 1950s, they brought ideas about how to mine coal at less cost than ever. By using huge modern equipment such as bulldozers and diesel-powered shovels and augers, they could get at the coal under the earth and use fewer workers in the process. There was no longer any need to drill deep shafts into the depths and send men down to dig the coal. Two new types of mining came into use—strip mining and auger mining.

Strip mining is done by stripping off the tops of hills and mountains in order to get rid of the trees and the soil and lay bare the veins of coal. In auger mining, a bulldozer clears off a bench, or shelf, of the mountainside to make a roadway for heavy machinery. Then a huge steel auger, a type of drilling machine, bores a row of holes into the coal seam and spews the coal out onto a conveyor.

Strip mining and auger mining have produced cheap fuel. In doing so, however, they have robbed the Appalachians of both human and natural resources. Forests have been destroyed; former farmland has been lost. Once-beautiful rocky streams carrying fresh, clear water down from the mountains are now filled with mud, and in rainy weather giant mudslides wash away more trees and any buildings that might be in their path. Fish and wildlife, as well as many people, have lost their homes. Mountain families have been robbed of two means of livelihood at once— farming and mining. Thus, many of the brightest and most ambitious of the young people have left the area in search of jobs.

It has been estimated that there is enough coal in the mountains of eastern Kentucky and Tennessee for mining to continue for another thousand years. Though a federal law that went into effect in 1978 requires strip-mine owners to reclaim the land destroyed by surface mining, most of the land lost before that time has not been reclaimed. Conservationists hope that better mining methods can be developed and that ways can be found to reclaim the once-beautiful Kentucky mountains.

OTHER EMPLOYMENT

Meanwhile, as the old ways are disappearing, all too often leaving much pain in their path, young Kentuckians are learning new life-styles and ways of earning a living.

In recent years, less than 10 percent of personal income in the state has come from farms and mines. The largest sources of income are manufacturing, government, wholesale and retail trade, and service industries.

Manufacturing in Kentucky is highly diversified, and jobs are spread out among many types of companies. No single type of manufacturer employs more than about 3 percent of the total work force engaged in that activity.

Goods produced in Kentucky include food; liquor, especially the bourbon for which Kentucky is famous; tobacco products; textiles; clothing; paper and paper products; printed materials; chemicals, including plastics and paints; petroleum and coal products; rubber products; and leather and leather products. These are classified as "nondurable goods." "Durable goods" include lumber and wood products; furniture and fixtures; machinery; electric and electronic equipment; transportation equipment; and products made of stone, clay, glass, and metals.

CRAFTS

Appalachian mountain people are known far and wide for their crafts—handmade items such as baskets, dolls and other toys, musical instruments, furniture, fabrics, quilts, and pottery. In pioneer days, it was essential to know how to make these items. People living in the isolated hollows had to make them themselves or do without.

Later on, by the end of the 1800s, factory-made goods began to be available in the mountains, and the traditional skills were not quite so necessary for survival. They were in danger of being forgotten as handcrafted goods became less and less valued and less and less plentiful.

Certain people from outside the highlands, especially teachers and missionaries, realized that the old crafts could be a source of income for many local people who were unemployed and unskilled, and encouraged their development.

Today, many shops in Kentucky are filled with fine native crafts. Some of the artisans learned the skills from their parents and grandparents; others have been trained in art classes at universities and private colleges such as Berea.

Chapter 8
HORSES

HORSES

Kentucky has had a love affair with horses for two hundred years.

In 1775, even before many settlers had come to the territory, Daniel Boone introduced a resolution in the Virginia legislature that called for improving the breed of horses in Kentucky County.

THE BLUEGRASS

The Bluegrass is truly horse country. Beautiful horse farms stretch out to the horizon for mile after mile. Kentucky's mild and temperate climate and the land of the Bluegrass are ideally suited for the raising of Thoroughbred horses. The terrain is gently rolling; the turf is dry and firm; there are open woods; and there is plenty of water. The limestone bedrock under the turf gives both the water and grass a high content of limestone and calcium—two elements that build strong bones, muscles, and tendons in the horses.

Kentucky's early settlers needed horses. They shipped them in along the rivers, on flatboats. Those first horses were strong and fast, and their owners started trading and breeding to develop even better strains.

A mare and her colt graze on a Lexington horse farm.

HORSE FARMS

Today, raising horses is big business in the Bluegrass. Large tracts of land are marked off by fences or old, mossy stone walls. Huge trees—elms, maples, and gnarled sycamores—shade the paddocks and meadows.

The inside of a horse barn is as clean as a ship. The horse stalls gleam with varnished wood and metal trim. Grooms care for the animals as if they were babies, making sure that their coats are kept clean and glossy and that they are well fed and properly exercised. Daily records are kept of everything the horses eat, as well as their temperatures and other facts relating to their health. Veterinarians are constantly on watch.

Brood mares foal, or give birth, in the spring. Newborns, or foals, are fed an excellent diet with plenty of vitamins. When they are a few weeks old, trainers get them accustomed to a halter. Training for racing begins when they are a year old.

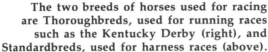
The two breeds of horses used for racing
are Thoroughbreds, used for running races
such as the Kentucky Derby (right), and
Standardbreds, used for harness races (above).

Three breeds of horses have been developed in Kentucky. Best known is the Thoroughbred, an ideal racehorse with a long, low, straight stride. Only horses whose ancestry can be traced and documented back to English Thoroughbreds of the 1770s qualify as Thoroughbreds. A foal must be registered with the Jockey Club, with its bloodline accurately recorded, in order to be called a Thoroughbred.

Some Thoroughbreds are used for polo, some as saddle horses or hunters. But every breeder hopes that at least one of his foals will grow up to be a great racehorse, and the attendants watch carefully for signs of potential stardom.

There are two main types of horse races—running races and harness races. Thoroughbreds belong to the class known as saddle horses. They were developed primarily for use in running races, to be ridden by jockeys. For harness racing, the horse is hitched to a small sulky. The driver sits on this small, two-wheeled carriage and holds the reins.

Harness racing requires horses with somewhat different characteristics from those of the Thoroughbred. A second breed developed in Kentucky, the Standardbred, is considered the best

for harness racing. There are two classes of Standardbreds—
trotters and pacers. They have great speed, stamina, and
endurance. The Standardbred was developed by crossing the
Thoroughbred with other types of horses.

A third breed—the American Saddle Horse—has also been
developed in Kentucky. This is a favorite with people who ride
horses for pleasure.

THE KENTUCKY DERBY

The Kentucky Derby, best known of all horse races held in the
United States, takes place in Louisville on the first Saturday of
each May. Churchill Downs, home of the Derby, is a 180-acre
(72.8-hectare) landscaped park. Its track is one of the fastest in the
world. It opened in 1875, and the first Derby was run that year.
Originally the race was a mile and a half long (nearly two and a
half kilometers); now it is a mile and a quarter (two kilometers).

The Kentucky Derby is truly a state-wide celebration. It has
been called the most spectacular two minutes in the entire sports
world. The grandstands hold about 42,000 people, and another
80,000 or so crowd into the park. It is one huge party within the
park, and all over the state other Kentuckians are holding Derby
parties, too, gathering together to watch the race on television.

In 1904, the tradition began of decorating the winning horse
with a blanket of roses, and in 1925 a sports columnist gave the
race a nickname it has had ever since—the Run for the Roses.

The Derby can be given credit for the development of the
breeding and raising of horses in Kentucky. As the race became
more and more famous, wealthy horse owners in other parts of
the United States began to buy huge tracts of land and move their
stables to the Bluegrass.

Chapter 9

CULTURE AND
RECREATION

CULTURE AND RECREATION

The Bluegrass is a geographic section of Kentucky. It is also a term used to describe a type of popular country music that was developed after the Second World War. A Kentucky musician, Bill Monroe, is given credit for initiating bluegrass music. He has explained it as a combination of jazz, traditional mountain fiddle music, and church music.

MOUNTAIN MUSIC

The mountain craftspeople of Kentucky made other articles besides the basic necessities of clothing, furniture, and utensils. Dolls, toys, and musical instruments were also homemade. Some of the first colonists brought fiddles and dulcimers with them from England. Skillful artisans learned to fashion new instruments copied from these originals.

A dulcimer, also called a mountain zither, is a stringed instrument that is plucked while being held on the lap of the musician. Dulcimers are always handmade, of beautiful woods, and come in many different shapes.

After the fiddle and the dulcimer came the banjo, which was at first a crude, primitive instrument made from gourds. These three were used by small groups of musicians who entertained at parties and square dances in the mountain hamlets. Later, in the twentieth century, the combos were enlarged to include guitars, mandolins, and bass viols.

In the early 1940s, traditional Kentucky mountain music became familiar to the rest of the country. Kentucky artisans still make such instruments as dulcimers (left), and bluegrass bands (above) perform at music festivals throughout the state.

Besides instruments, the mountain people brought the old English and Scottish ballads with them to the southern highlands. In the 1920s and 1930s, several music researchers and historians "discovered" mountain music. They traveled into the tiny settlements and made records of the old hymns and folk songs.

In 1939, a radio broadcast called the Renfro Valley Barn Dance was started in a pretty little Kentucky village about fifty miles (eighty kilometers) south of Lexington. Within a couple of years, the show was syndicated, and people all over the United States became familiar with Kentucky mountain music.

Today, Renfro Valley is a major country music center. It hosts thousands of visitors who come to see and hear the Barn Dance show and other musical performances. Several popular music festivals are also held each summer in other communities—Berea, Lexington, and Olive Hill, for example.

Scottish musical traditions are kept alive at an annual Kentucky Scottish Weekend in Carrollton. Bagpipe bands and highland dancers provide the entertainment.

OTHER PERFORMING ARTS

Louisville, Kentucky's largest city, is a center for the lively arts. The Kentucky Center for the Performing Arts is a beautiful modern showcase and home of the Louisville Orchestra, the Kentucky Opera, the Louisville Ballet, the Broadway Series, and Stage One: Children's Theater. The building itself is spectacular. Besides the resident arts companies, the center hosts concerts by visiting artists, including classical orchestras, country music bands, jazz bands, and big bands.

Concerts and other performances are also offered in the Louisville Palace. This is a renovated movie house built in the 1920s, the heyday of elaborate, ornate theater architecture.

Lexington, too, supports music, and the city has its own Philharmonic Orchestra. For contrast, each summer a Festival of the Bluegrass is held in Lexington's 680-acre (275-hectare) Masterson Station Park, featuring the particular type of country folk music that has taken its name from the region. More than twenty bands perform for the festival.

Actors Theatre of Louisville has a national reputation for excellence. In addition to regular performances of classical and well-recognized modern plays, Actors Theatre specializes in first performances of new plays.

Free performances of Shakespeare plays are presented by a professional theater company in Louisville's Central Park during the summer.

Summer-stock theater is offered at the Pioneer Playhouse in Danville and Thomas Opera House in Horse Cave. Several Kentucky cities have dinner theaters.

Colleges and universities throughout the state have regular seasons of performing arts and spectator sports.

According to local legend, Stephen Foster (left) was inspired to write "My Old Kentucky Home" when he was visiting this estate near Bardstown (above).

Outdoor historic dramas at three locations in Kentucky bring part of the area's past to life each summer. An amphitheater in Harrodsburg is the setting for two of them. *The Legend of Daniel Boone* is a thriller based on the exploits of Boone and other men and women who first ventured westward into the wilderness to settle a new land. *Lincoln* starts with the early days of the sixteenth president of the United States, dramatizing his rise to the White House as well as the tragic years of the Civil War.

The Stephen Foster Story attracts huge crowds to Bardstown to enjoy the nightly performances of a muscial. Stephen Foster, who wrote many popular songs, never actually lived in Kentucky. However, he probably did visit an estate near Bardstown several times, and his song "My Old Kentucky Home" has made Kentuckians regard him as an adopted son of the state.

Shakertown Revisited, performed each summer in South Union, retells the story of the unusual group of people who founded communities in Kentucky based on their religious beliefs. While there are no Shakers left in the state today, their legacy of thrift, hard work, and craftsmanship is an important part of Kentucky's heritage.

A Kentuckian of great renown in the field of motion pictures was David W. Griffith. A pioneer movie maker, he produced the epic *Birth of a Nation* and in 1936 was awarded a special Oscar for his achievements.

LITERATURE

A number of Kentucky writers have drawn inspiration from the beauty and tragedy of their native state, especially the eastern, mountainous part.

Jesse Stuart, who wrote poems, novels, and short stories about Kentucky, published more than two hundred short stories within twenty years.

Robert Penn Warren wrote several books about violence in the history of the South. He won two Pulitzer Prizes, one in 1947 for the novel *All the King's Men,* and the second for poetry, in 1957. Two of his well-known novels were based on incidents in Kentucky history: *World Enough and Time* and *The Cave.* In 1986, Warren was appointed the first poet laureate of the United States.

John William Fox, Jr. wrote best-selling novels about the Cumberland mountaineers and the aristocrats of the Bluegrass. Two of his best-known books were made into movies—*The Little Shepherd of Kingdom Come* and *The Trail of the Lonesome Pine.*

Harriet Arnow, Janice Holt Giles, and Rebecca Caudill have produced several books, both fiction and nonfiction, based on their experiences in the area. Elizabeth Madox Roberts also used Kentucky settings for her novels. Harry M. Caudill is one of eastern Kentucky's most eloquent spokespersons about the destruction of natural resources by reckless methods of mining and forestry.

Alice Hegan Rice wrote books that were popular with children

Craft items such as baskets, custom-made furniture, hand-loomed blankets, pottery, and handmade quilts are an important part of Kentucky's tradition.

a generation or two ago: *Mrs. Wiggs of the Cabbage Patch* and *A Romance of Billy Goat Hill.*

Paducah-born Irvin S. Cobb was an actor and screen writer in Hollywood. He was also distinguished in the areas of journalism and the writing of humorous pieces, short stories, and novels. His attitude of poking fun at himself and at life is obvious in the title of his autobiography, *Exit Laughing.*

FOLK ARTS

As mentioned earlier, handcrafts are an important part of Kentucky's tradition. In recent years, outsiders have discovered the beauty, high quality, and distinctiveness of many of these items. Handmade quilts are sold for good prices, as are custom-made items of furniture, hand-loomed blankets, and woolen clothing.

The Kentucky Shakers made beautifully simple pieces of furniture. Their living quarters were plain, with no unnecessary objects, but their chairs, tables, and cupboards were excellently designed and made of the finest woods. Other Kentuckians were influenced by the Shakers' work.

Handcrafted dolls are made of such readily available materials as corn husks, nuts, and dried fruits. Simple toys are whittled out of wood.

Shops selling locally made crafts are plentiful in Kentucky, and many crafts fairs are held throughout the summer months in major cities, smaller villages, and many state parks and other recreational areas.

SPORTS

Basketball is the favorite sport in eastern Kentucky. Nearly every high school in the state has a gymnasium and a basketball team.

Two of Kentucky's college basketball teams, the Wildcats of the University of Kentucky at Lexington and the Cardinals of the University of Louisville, are frequent contenders and sometimes champions in national collegiate tournaments. The two teams are fierce rivals.

Kentuckians are fanatic boosters of local basketball teams. Since 1982, the University of Kentucky has sold tickets to the Wildcats' first practice session of the season, and all twelve thousand seats in Memorial Coliseum are always filled!

The University of Kentucky Wildcats (left), and the University of Louisville Cardinals, fierce rivals, have some of the most ardent fans in college basketball.

Kentucky Wesleyan, a smaller college located in Owensboro, has held the top spot in their division several times.

The state's love affair with horses is obvious in the large crowds that show up to watch horse races, harness races, steeplechases, and other events. Louisville's Churchill Downs and Lexington's Keeneland Race Course are major racing centers.

Baseball fans cross the Ohio River to root for the Cincinnati Reds, or go to Louisville to see the Redbirds, a AAA minor-league team.

An Olympic-style sports competition for amateur athletes, the Bluegrass State Games, is held each summer. Most events are held in Lexington, though a few are held in Louisville, Frankfort, Georgetown, and Richmond. Hundreds of competitors are involved in archery, bowling, canoeing, cycling, diving, equestrian competition, gymnastics, roller skating, shooting, soccer, softball, swimming, tennis, track and field, and volleyball.

Chapter 10
TOURING THE BLUEGRASS STATE

TOURING THE BLUEGRASS STATE

People who vacation in Kentucky can find a lot of variety in things to see and do: beautiful scenery, plenty of opportunities for outdoor sports, historic sightseeing, and much more.

THE LOUISVILLE AREA

Louisville is the state's largest city, with a population of about 300,000. It is lively and attractive. Its location on the south bank of the Ohio River, beside the only falls in the river, has influenced its growth from the very beginning. One of the earliest settlements in Kentucky, it was founded in 1788. It gained commercial prominence first as a shipping center for river traffic, and then later for rail, highway, and air transportation.

In the 1970s and 1980s, Louisville has seen some major facelifting in its downtown area. New and exciting modern architecture has been used for such structures as Founders Square, the Galleria, and the Kentucky Center. At the same time, a number of lovely older buildings have been renovated, giving visual variety to the new stretches of glass and steel.

A vacation spent in and around Louisville can be full of variety. A cruise on the sternwheeler riverboat *Belle of Louisville* gives first-time visitors a good look at the city from the river. Anyone who likes horses will want to visit the Kentucky Derby Museum at Churchill Downs.

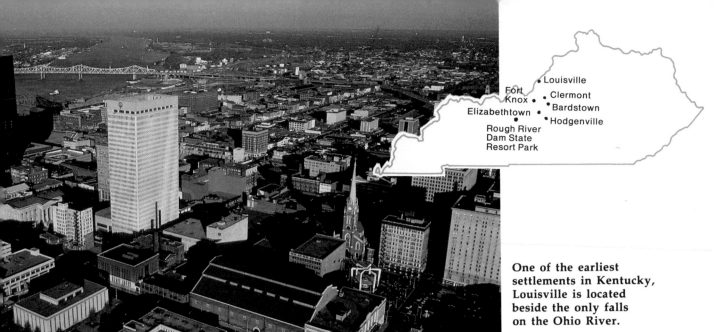

One of the earliest settlements in Kentucky, Louisville is located beside the only falls on the Ohio River.

The man who founded the Kentucky Fried Chicken company was from Louisville, and a movie about his life and how he climbed from poverty to wealth is shown regularly at the Colonel Harland Sanders Museum.

Another museum that is unusual and fun is the Kentucky Railway Museum, with its collection of train cars and engines from all periods of railway history. Louisville also has a fine zoo, botanical gardens, art museums, a museum of history and science, a planetarium, and several historic house museums.

The Patton Museum of Cavalry and Armor is at Fort Knox, just a few miles south of Louisville. Though no one is permitted to view the gold kept at Fort Knox, the Patton Museum is open to everyone. The collection includes mementos of General Patton's army career, as well as a collection of military tanks and weapons.

Nearby, in Elizabethtown, is Schmidt's Coca-Cola Museum, a huge collection of Coca-Cola memorabilia—such items as a soda

The one-room cabin in which Abraham Lincoln was born is now enclosed in a memorial building (right). The reconstructed home in which he spent his boyhood (above) is only a few miles away.

fountain from the 1890s, a three-foot tall Coke bottle, and the world's largest collection of Coca-Cola trays.

Also in Elizabethtown is the Lincoln Heritage House—really two log houses. Abraham Lincoln's father helped build these, and they are furnished with items of the days when Lincoln was young.

Thirteen miles (twenty-one kilometers) south of here, in Hodgenville, are more sites connected with Lincoln. The one-room log cabin in which historians believe Lincoln was born has been enclosed within a granite and marble memorial building, to keep it protected from the weather. An audiovisual show is presented in the visitors center, and there are exhibits related to Lincoln's life.

The Lincoln family moved away from this house when Abe was only two-and-a-half years old, and spent the next six years in a cabin about ten miles (sixteen kilometers) away from his birthplace. This cabin has been reconstructed and furnished with antiques and historic items. It is open to the public during spring and summer. Each Saturday night in Hodgenville, country music performers put on a Lincoln Jamboree—a very popular show.

West of Hodgenville is Rough River Dam State Resort Park, one of Kentucky's outstanding state resort parks. These parks have lodges and cottages for rent as well as camping sites. Rough River Lake, a large lake formed by a dam on the river, is one of the best fishing lakes in the state; it is equally popular for houseboating, water skiing, and other water sports.

Each July, the Official Kentucky State Championship Old Time Fiddlers Contest is held at Rough River Dam Park, and top musicians from all over the country come to take part.

Southeast of Louisville is Bardstown, where song writer Stephen Foster used to visit his cousins. A beautiful mansion built almost two hundred years ago was the inspiration for the song "My Old Kentucky Home." The mansion is now preserved in My Old Kentucky Home State Park, where the musical *The Stephen Foster Story* is presented in an outdoor amphitheater on summer evenings.

St. Joseph's Cathedral in Bardstown, the first Catholic cathedral built west of the Allegheny Mountains, contains a collection of priceless paintings donated by King Louis Philippe of France. Stone Castle Museum, also in Bardstown, houses a collection of five thousand toy soldiers from all over the world—most of them handmade and very valuable. They are displayed in dioramas.

A beautiful spot for a picnic is the Bernheim Forest Arboretum and Nature Center in Clermont, between Bardstown and Louisville. In this large, wooded wildlife refuge with ornamental gardens, nature trails, ponds, and a museum, more than seventeen hundred varieties of plants are labeled.

The centerpiece of this aerial view of Covington is the Cathedral Basilica of the Assumption, which has one of the largest stained-glass windows in the world.

COVINGTON AND NORTHERN KENTUCKY

Going northeast from Louisville along the Ohio River, one comes to Covington, Kentucky's fourth-largest city. An interesting stop on the way to Covington is Big Bone Lick State Park, near Union. In prehistoric times, this area was a swampland containing a great supply of salt. Large herds of giant mastodons, mammoths, bison, and other animals congregated here, attracted by the salt. When they stepped into the oozing swamps, however, they became trapped and died. Hundreds of bones of these animals have been found here; many of them were collected in the late 1700s and early 1800s and taken to museums throughout the United States and Europe. Quite a few are displayed in the park's museum.

In Fort Mitchell, between Union and Covington, the Vent Haven Museum has more than five hundred ventriloquist figures on display.

Covington, across the river from Cincinnati, Ohio, is linked to it by three broad bridges, and is a part of the greater Cincinnati

Looking across a riverboat restaurant in Covington to the Cincinnati skyline

metropolitan area. A large restoration area in West Covington, called Main Strasse Village, reflects the German heritage of the area. A 100-foot (30.4-meter) bell tower houses a carillon, played each hour. On the tower is an animated clock with twenty-one mechanical figures that perform the story of the Pied Piper of Hamelin. Horse-drawn carriages make tours of this and other Covington neighborhoods, and boats conduct sightseeing cruises on the river.

South of Covington, at Falmouth, is Adam's Buffalo Farm, where visitors are welcome to watch the buffalo roam. Nearby is Blue Licks Battlefield State Park, an area important during more than one stage of the area's history. It was a salt lick, like Big Bone Park, where prehistoric mammoths met. Daniel Boone came here, also in search of salt, and was captured by Indians. And it was the site of the last battle of the revolutionary war, in 1782.

Lexington, Kentucky's
second-largest city,
was named for the 1775
Battle of Lexington.

IN THE HEART OF THE BLUEGRASS

Another concentration of places for good sightseeing is the
Lexington area. Lexington is Kentucky's second-largest city and
one of the oldest, dating from a camp named for the Battle of
Lexington (Massachusetts), in 1775. There is a large historic area
in Lexington, with beautiful and well-preserved homes built in
the early 1800s. Several are open to the public as house museums,
including the homes of Henry Clay and Mary Todd, who later
became Mrs. Abraham Lincoln.

The Red Mile Track is in Lexington. Keeneland Race Course and
the Kentucky Horse Park, near Lexington, are other attractions for
horse lovers. There visitors are permitted to watch horses being
given their workouts early each morning.

The Kentucky Horse Park is especially interesting. In 1972, the
commonwealth purchased a large farm at the edge of Lexington
for development as a state park. The farm had a long history.
Thoroughbreds had been bred on the farm since the 1840s.

Cross-country obstacle races are among the special events held at Kentucky Horse Park.

Kentucky Horse Park is unlike any other park in the world. Almost anything related to horses can be seen here. Visitors can tour the grounds in horse-drawn surreys or wagons, watch horses doing the kind of farm work they did in the 1800s, see a number of different breeds of horses and learn about their individual characteristics, and watch special horse events.

Quite a few horses reside temporarily at Kentucky Horse Park— on loan from their owners. There are representatives of more than thirty breeds. Some of the horses are put through their paces in a Parade of Breeds held two or three times each day. The Hall of Champions is a horse barn where visitors can get a look at several great racehorses.

Displays at the International Museum of the Horse include the Sears collection of hundreds of miniature horses and carriages, and more than five hundred gold and silver trophies won during a fifty-year period by the horses of Calumet Farm.

The American Saddle Horse Museum is also on the grounds, and other specialized museums will be added in the future.

Special events held at Kentucky Horse Park nearly every weekend include polo games, horse shows, rodeos, and steeplechases.

Weisenberger Mill, in Midway, has been processing meal and flour since 1865.

South of Frankfort, in the lovely horse country of the Bluegrass, the National Audubon Society operates the Buckley Wildlife Sanctuary. There are nature trails, a museum, and areas for birdwatching.

Nearby, at Midway, is Weisenberger Mill, the oldest commercial mill in the state. Meal and flour have been processed here since 1865.

Frankfort, the state capital, has a state history museum, a state military history museum, and other state buildings. A mini-zoo is located just west of Frankfort.

Southwest of Lexington is Harrodsburg, site of Kentucky's first permanent white settlement. Right in the center of town is a full-scale reproduction of Old Fort Harrod. Historical dramas are presented here in the summer.

Near Harrodsburg is Shaker Village at Pleasant Hill, where twenty-seven original buildings have been preserved. Costumed interpreters and artisans demonstrate the way of life of the unusual religious community that founded the village. The *Dixie Belle* riverboat makes sightseeing cruises on the Kentucky River.

Another Lincoln landmark is in Springfield, the boyhood home of Abraham's father, Thomas.

Students of Civil War history like to visit the Perryville Battlefield State Shrine, site of the fiercest battle fought in Kentucky during that war.

Danville was the capital of Kentucky while it was still a district of Virginia. Ten conventions were held here to form the state's constitution. In the center of town is an authentic reproduction of Kentucky's first courthouse square, along with original and recreated early buildings.

At Fort Boonesborough State Park, just south of Lexington, is a recreation of the fort built by Daniel Boone in 1775. Life of the earliest pioneers is demonstrated and illustrated through films and exhibits. There are paddlewheel excursions on the river.

Farther south is Berea, home of Berea College. On campus is the Appalachian Museum, where many traditional crafts are demonstrated.

EASTERN KENTUCKY AND THE MOUNTAINS

Interstate 64 east of Lexington leads to the Carter and Cascade Caves region of eastern Kentucky. Within Carter Caves State Resort Park are more than twenty caverns. Guided tours are conducted daily through five of them. One is called Bat Cave; it is the protected home of the social bat, which is on the United States list of vanishing species.

Farther east is the small city of Ashland, near the point where three states—Ohio, West Virginia, and Kentucky—meet. Much of the Appalachian heritage is preserved for visitors to enjoy and learn about in Ashland. Kentucky's noted author and one-time poet laureate, Jesse Stuart, lived ten miles (sixteen kilometers)

Jenny Wiley State Resort Park (above) and
the Breaks of the Sandy (right) are two of the
most picturesque areas in eastern Kentucky.

north of the city. His land is set aside as a nature preserve with
numerous hiking trails.

The Jean Thomas Museum and Cultural Center is the work of a
woman who spent her life collecting artifacts and examples of
Appalachian folk art. She was particularly interested in the old
folk songs handed down through generations of Appalachian
families. The displays include musical instruments, records,
furniture, paintings, and rare photographs.

The Kentucky Highlands Museum, in a mansion built by a
turn-of-the-century coal tycoon, displays Indian artifacts,
industrial exhibits, and memorabilia of the area.

The valley of the Big Sandy River flows along the eastern part
of Kentucky's Appalachian Mountains, entering Kentucky from
Virginia through a cut known as the Breaks of the Sandy. From
there it flows northward to the Ohio River near Ashland. This is
the territory explored by Daniel Boone, and the region where
pioneer woman Jenny Wiley lived in the wilds after escaping from

This huge natural arch gave Natural Bridge State Resort Park its name.

Indian captivity. It is also the home of the infamous, feuding Hatfields and McCoys. Many mountain music and crafts festivals are held here in the summer. There are three state parks in or near the valley. Hikers enjoy exploring the 100-mile (161-kilometer) Jenny Wiley hiking trail across mountain streams and along the tops of ridges.

At the edge of Kentucky's eastern mountains is a long strip that is colored green on most road maps. The Daniel Boone National Forest stretches all the way south to the Tennessee line. High on a hilltop, 3 miles (4.8 kilometers) from the Mountain Parkway, is a huge natural sandstone arch called the Natural Bridge. The arch is 78 feet (23.7 meters) wide and 65 feet (19.8 meters) high. Hikers climb to the top for a spectacular view; less rugged people take a skylift to see the panorama.

The Natural Bridge State Park is close to the Red River Gorge Geological Area, where there are more than fifty other natural arches, as well as steep cliffs, spires, pinnacles, and palisades.

Cumberland Falls, near Corbin, is the second-largest waterfall east of the Rocky Mountains; only Niagara Falls is larger.

South of Berea, on the edge of the national forest, is Renfro Valley, home of the Renfro Valley Country Music Center. Stage shows are presented every weekend from March through November, and there are frequent special events, such as square dances, Bluegrass music festivals, and talent contests.

The Great Saltpeter Cave at Livingston, discovered in 1789, was an important source of saltpeter, used in the manufacture of gunpowder. There are guided tours through the cave.

Levi Jackson State Park, near London, was the site of a bloody battle between early settlers and Indians in 1784. The Mountain Life Museum has a group of rustic cabins and farm buildings with pioneer relics, farm tools, and early household furnishings.

Cumberland Falls, near Corbin, is probably the single most spectacular natural sight in the state of Kentucky. It is the second-largest waterfall east of the Rockies; only Niagara is larger. For three or four nights each month around the time of the full moon, if all the weather conditions are right, a moonbow can be seen in the mist of the falls. As far as is known, this happens in only one other place in the world—Victoria Falls, in Africa. Many people like to go river rafting in the Cumberland River Gorge below the falls.

Twenty-three miles (37 kilometers) south of Corbin is a replica of the first pioneer cabin in Kentucky, a one-room log house built by Dr. Thomas Walker. Walker, Daniel Boone, and other pioneers came into Kentucky from Virginia through Cumberland Gap, a natural passage in the mountains. Cumberland Gap is at the point where Virginia, Tennessee, and Kentucky meet. Nearly 32 square miles (82.8 square kilometers) of the land surrounding the pass are a part of the National Park System. There are two caves under the park and 50 miles (80.4 kilometers) of hiking trails.

SOUTH-CENTRAL KENTUCKY AND THE CAVES

Bowling Green is the largest city in south-central Kentucky and the commercial and cultural center of the region. It is an industrial town, a college town, and an agricultural trading center.

A million and a half visitors come to this part of Kentucky each year to see one of the wonders of the world—Mammoth Cave. It is the largest cave system in the world, with 300 miles (483 kilometers) of mapped passageways. Several different guided cave tours are conducted by Park Service rangers. A riverboat takes visitors on cruises through scenic parts of the park.

Other caves in the area can also be explored: Crystal Onyx Cave at Cave City, containing a large Indian burial ground; Diamond Caverns; Hundred Dome Cave; and Jesse James Cave, in Park City. Jesse James and his gang are believed to have used this last one as a hideout.

Some of Kentucky's loveliest state parks are in the region, boasting fine fishing in their lakes and streams.

WESTERN KENTUCKY AND THE LAND BETWEEN THE LAKES

Owensboro is Kentucky's third-largest city, but it is quite a bit smaller than Louisville and Lexington. Located on the Ohio River, it is the major hub of western Kentucky. Owensboro has three colleges, a symphony orchestra, a theater workshop, and many beautiful old homes. Each summer, a four-day Great Ohio River Flatboat Race is held; the boats go from Owensboro to Henderson.

Near Henderson is the John James Audubon State Park, a wooded area for picnicking and camping where many songbirds live. Audubon, the noted painter of nature subjects—especially birds—lived in the area for several years and painted the native warblers. A museum in the park has a priceless collection of 126 original prints from his collection *The Birds of America*, published in 1826.

The Ohio River flows into the Mississippi near Wickliffe, Kentucky. This was the site of an ancient city of the Mississippian Culture.

A few miles south along the Mississippi River is the Columbus-Belmont Battlefield, where a major skirmish of the Civil War took place.

The two huge lakes formed by TVA dams, Kentucky Lake and Lake Barkley, have created Kentucky's most popular resort and vacationing area. The 40-mile (64.4-kilometer) peninsula between the two lakes is one of the largest outdoor recreation areas in the United States. Its appropriate, but not very imaginative, name is Land Between the Lakes.

Camping, fishing, hiking, swimming, boating—all sorts of outdoor activities—are available. A huge environmental-education center has a living-history farm where chores are done as they were in 1850. At a demonstration farm, visitors can learn about

Kentucky Lake (left) and Lake Barkley, two huge lakes formed by TVA dams, created the Land Between the Lakes, one of the state's most popular resort areas.

contemporary agricultural methods. A herd of buffalo lives nearby.

In the small village of Fairview, a few miles east of Lake Barkley, Jefferson Davis, president of the Confederate States of America, was born. A tall concrete monument to his memory overlooks a replica of the log house in which he was born.

From the mountain streams to the Mississippi delta, from the cities of the Bluegrass to the hamlets of the Pennyroyal, Kentucky's people share a pride in their rich pioneer heritage and a strong love for their lovely land. But remember, one interpretation of the original Indian name for the territory is ''land of tomorrow.'' Kentuckians believe this. They're not living in the past, they're moving forward confidently toward the future.

107

FACTS AT A GLANCE

GENERAL INFORMATION

Statehood: June 1, 1792, fifteenth state

Origin of Name: The official name is Commonwealth of Kentucky. Commonwealth literally means "for the good of all," but at the time the name was adopted, the words state and commonwealth were synonymous. Several Indian groups had a word for this region that sounded like "Kentucky," each with a different interpretation. Several translations have been recorded, including "dark and bloody ground," "great meadows," and "land of tomorrow."

State Capital: Frankfort, founded 1786

State Nickname: "Bluegrass State," from the lush, dark grass that is common in the state. The grass derives its name from the bluish-purple buds that bloom in the spring and make whole meadows and lawns look blue.

State Flag: In the center of the Kentucky-blue flag is a replica of the state seal: In a circle of white, bordered in gold, are shown two men shaking hands with each other and the state motto, "United we stand, divided we fall," to symbolize brotherhood. Below the circle are two branches of goldenrod, the state flower, in green and gold; above the circle, lettered in gold, is the state name, Commonwealth of Kentucky.

State Motto: "United we stand; divided we fall"

State Bird: Kentucky cardinal

State Animal: Gray squirrel

State Flower: Goldenrod

State Tree: Kentucky coffee tree

State Fish: Kentucky bass

State Song: "My Old Kentucky Home," words and music by Stephen Collins Foster, adopted as the official state song in 1928:

The sun shines bright on my old Kentucky home,
'Tis summer, the old folks are gay;
The corn-top's ripe and the meadow's in the bloom,
While the birds make music all the day.
The young folks roll on the little cabin floor,
All merry, all happy and bright,
By'n by hard times comes a-knocking at the door,
Then, my old Kentucky home, good-night!

Weep no more, my lady, Oh! weep no more today!
We will sing one song for the old Kentucky Home,
For the old Kentucky Home, far away.

They hunt no more for the 'possum and the coon,
On the meadow, the hill, and the shore;
They sing no more by the glimmer of the moon,
On the bench by the old cabin door.
The day goes by like a shadow o'er the heart,
With sorrow, where all was delight:
The time has come when the old folks have to part;
Then my old Kentucky Home, good-night!

Weep no more, my lady, Oh! weep no more today!
We will sing one song for the old Kentucky Home,
For the old Kentucky Home, far away.

The head must bow, and the back will have to bend,
Wherever the old folks may go:
A few more days, and the trouble all will end,
In the field where the sugarcanes grow.
A few more days for to tote the weary load,
No matter, 'twill never be light,
A few more days till we totter on the road;
Then my old Kentucky Home, good-night!

Weep no more, my lady, Oh! weep no more today!
We will sing one song for the old Kentucky Home,
For the old Kentucky Home, far away.

POPULATION

Population: 3,660,257, twenty-third among the states (1980 census)

Population Density: 90.6 people per sq. mi. (34.9 per km²)

Population Distribution: By 1970, for the first time in the state's history, more Kentucky citizens were living in cities and towns than on farms and in rural areas. Now, nearly 25 percent of Kentucky's people live in the state's twelve largest cities, and about 15 percent live in the urban areas of Louisville and Lexington.

Louisville	298,694
Lexington	204,165
Owensboro	54,450
Covington	49,574
Bowling Green	40,450
Paducah	29,315
Hopkinsville	27,318
Ashland	27,064
Frankfort	25,973
Henderson	24,834
Richmond	21,705
Newport	21,587

(Population figures according to 1980 census)

Population Growth: Kentucky's population continues to grow, but at a slower rate than that of the country as a whole. The list below shows the state's population growth since 1790:

Year	Population
1790	73,677
1800	220,955
1810	406,511
1820	564,317
1830	687,917
1840	779,828
1850	982,405
1860	1,155,684
1870	1,321,011
1880	1,648,690
1890	1,858,635
1900	2,147,174
1910	2,289,905
1920	2,416,630
1930	2,614,589
1940	2,845,627
1950	2,944,806
1960	3,038,156
1970	3,220,711
1980	3,660,257

The Cumberland River cuts through the Big South Fork National River and Recreation Area, which straddles the Kentucky-Tennessee border.

GEOGRAPHY

Borders: Rivers form Kentucky's borders on the west, north, and northeast. The Mississippi River is the western border, with the state of Missouri on the other side. Across the Ohio River, which forms the northern border, are the three states of Ohio, Indiana, and Illinois. The big Sandy River and the Tug Fork, on the northeast, separate the state from West Virginia. Virginia borders Kentucky in the mountainous southeast, and Tennessee lies along the state's entire southern border.

Highest Point: Black Mountain, in Harlan County, 4,145 ft. (1,263 m) above sea level

Lowest Point: In Fulton County, on the Mississippi River, 257 ft. (78 m) above sea level

Greatest Distances: East to west, 350 mi. (563 km);
North to south, 175 mi. (282 km)

Area: 40,395 sq. mi. (104,623 km²)

Rank in Area Among the States: Thirty-seventh

Rivers: Kentucky is especially blessed with rivers. According to the United States Corps of Engineers, Kentucky has more miles of navigable waterways than any other state except Alaska. The Mississippi, Ohio, Big Sandy, and Tug Fork form the western, northern, and northeastern borders. Some of the principal rivers within the state are the Cumberland, Green, Kentucky, Licking, Salt, Tennessee, Tradewater, and Barren.

Lakes: Most of Kentucky's lakes have been created by dams in the rivers. The dams were constructed to provide flood control, hydroelectric energy, and soil and water conservation. The lakes and surrounding areas are also popular recreational lands. Some of the major lakes are Barkley, Barren River, Cave Run, Cumberland, Dale Hollow, Grayson, Green River, Herrington, Kentucky, Nolin River, Rough River, Taylorsville, Carr Fork, Buckhorn, Fishtrap, Dewey, Paintsville, and Malone.

Topography: Kentucky has great variety in topography. Most geographers divide the state into the following six regions: the Eastern Kentucky Coal Field, a rugged, mountainous, forested area with many streams; the Bluegrass region in the north-central part of the state, an area of gently rolling terrain; the Knobs, a chain of low hills running in a half-circle south of the Bluegrass; the Pennyroyal Plateau, another region of gently rolling terrain covering much of the southwestern part of the state; the Western Kentucky Coal Field, a hilly area in the western part of the state that is less rugged than the Eastern Coal Field and is bounded on the north by the Ohio River, south of Indiana and Illinois; and the Jackson Purchase, a low, flat plain in the extreme western part of the state.

Climate: Kentucky's climate is temperate, with moderate temperatures during all seasons. Extremes of heat and cold are rare. Ordinarily, there is ample rainfall during warm months and a small amount of snowfall in winter. Mountainous areas experience more snow and colder temperatures. The average temperature in January is 38° F. (3° C). In July, the state's average temperature is 77.5° F. (25.3° C). The highest recorded temperature was 114° F. (46° C) at Greensburg on July 28, 1930. The lowest was -34° F. (-37° C) at Cynthiana on January 28, 1963.

NATURE

Trees: Kentucky coffee tree, tulip tree, white oak, red oak, white pine, sycamore, ash, beech, maple, walnut, hemlock, red cedar

Wild Plants: Goldenrod, red clover, field daisy, black-eyed Susan, mountain laurel, rhododendron, dogwood, redbud, magnolia, trillium, fern, violet

Animals: Gray squirrel, white-tailed deer, bobcat, groundhog, raccoon, fox, opossum, rabbit, bat

Birds: Kentucky cardinal, wild turkey, wild ducks, wild geese, American egret, great blue heron, bobwhite, mourning dove, house sparrow

Fish: Bass, bluegill, trout, catfish, crappie, muskellunge, rockfish, walleye

GOVERNMENT

Kentucky has three branches of government—executive, judicial, and legislative. Executive officials include the governor, lieutenant governor, secretary of state, auditor, attorney general, treasurer, commissioner of agriculture, superintendent of public instruction, auditor of public accounts, and the three members of the railroad commission. All of these are elected for four-year terms and may not serve two consecutive terms.

The executive branch, headed by the governor, administers the law. The governor has the authority to veto or approve laws passed by the General Assembly, to grant pardons, to serve as commander-in-chief of the state militia unless it has been called into federal service, to call emergency sessions of the General Assembly, and to appoint many state administrators.

The legislative branch—the General Assembly—consists of a thirty-eight-member senate and a one-hundred-member house of representatives. The state is divided into thirty-eight senatorial districts and one hundred representative districts, all as equal in population as possible.

A state senator must be at least thirty years old, a citizen of Kentucky, and must have lived in the state at least six years immediately preceding his election. He must have lived in his district for at least one year prior to election. Senators are elected for four-year terms, with half the senate elected every two years. A state representative must be at least twenty-four years old, a citizen of Kentucky, and must have lived in the state for at least two years and in his district for one year prior to election. Representatives are elected for two-year terms, with the entire house elected at the same time.

Officers of the house and senate are elected by the members of the legislative bodies, with the exception of the president of the senate, an office held by the lieutenant governor of the state.

The General Assembly meets in Frankfort on the first Tuesday after the first Monday in January of even-numbered years. Sessions may not last more than sixty legislative days and may not extend beyond April 15. Special sessions may be called by the governor to deal with specific subjects; these are usually brief.

The judicial branch interprets the laws and tries cases. All members of Kentucky's judicial branch are elected by popular vote. There are four levels of courts in Kentucky: district courts, circuit courts, the court of appeals, and the supreme court. The supreme court hears all appeals of severe sentences—from twenty years or more of imprisonment to death—and such other cases as it may decide to hear. All judges in Kentucky must be attorneys and are elected for eight-year terms, except district judges, who are elected for four years.

Number of Counties: 120

U.S. Representatives: 7

Electoral Votes: 9

Voting Qualifications: Eighteen years of age, must have been registered with the county of residence for thirty days

EDUCATION

Each of Kentucky's 120 counties is a separate school district. There are also independent public school systems within these counties. Currently, Kentucky has 178 school districts. All children between the ages of seven and sixteen must attend school. About 10 percent of the state's school-age children attend parochial and private schools.

Kentucky has twenty-four senior colleges and universities, five junior colleges, and thirteen community colleges. The largest universities, by number of students, are the University of Kentucky, Lexington; the University of Louisville, Louisville; Eastern Kentucky University, Richmond; and Western Kentucky University, Bowling Green.

Among the oldest and most prominent of the independent colleges are Transylvania University, Lexington; Berea College, Berea; and Centre College, Danville. Transylvania was chartered in 1780 and is the oldest college west of the Allegheny Mountains. Berea College was established in 1855 and chartered in 1866. It is dedicated to providing an excellent education for the young people of eastern Kentucky without regard to their ability to pay; it operates on a tuition-free work-study plan. Centre College, another fine liberal-arts school, was established in 1819.

There are fourteen state vocational-technical schools and seventy-two area vocational education centers in the state.

KET, Kentucky's educational television network, covers the entire state as well as parts of five adjoining states. Programs include series for use in classrooms, a general educational-development program leading to a high-school diploma, courses offering college credit, children's programs, and cultural and public affairs programs.

ECONOMY AND INDUSTRY

Principal Products
Agriculture: Tobacco, horses and mules, hogs, cattle, dairy products, soybeans, corn, hay, wheat, barley, and rye

Manufacturing: Machinery; transportation equipment; electrical and electronic equipment; food products, including bourbon whiskey, meat products, soft drinks, and bakery products; tobacco products; chemicals and allied products; printing and publishing

Mining: Bituminous and lignite coal, petroleum, limestone, natural gas

Communication: Louisville has the newspaper with the largest circulation in the state—the *Courier-Journal*. Next is the *Lexington Herald-Leader*. There are more than twenty daily newspapers circulated in the state; most are regional in nature and have a small circulation. Each of the 120 counties has at least one weekly. There are eleven commercial television stations plus the Kentucky Educational Television network. It is estimated that 90 percent of the homes in the state have at least one television set.

A pioneer cabin exhibit in Frankfort's Kentucky State Historical Museum

Transportation: The two earliest routes of travel in Kentucky were the Wilderness Road and the Ohio River. The Wilderness Road was a route for the export of livestock well into the twentieth century.

The third major route was the north-south path between Louisville and Nashville. The L & N Railroad was built along this path and was a significant factor in the development of trade between Louisville and southern markets. Today Interstate routes I-65 and I-75 are major north-south arteries.

There are nearly 70,000 mi. (112,654 km) of highways in the state and 1,090 mi. (1,754 km) of commercially navigable waterways. The Tennessee-Tombigbee Waterway, now nearing completion, will reduce travel time by water between Kentucky and the Gulf of Mexico by as much as five days. There are seven public river ports in Kentucky and two more under development.

Nineteen rail carriers transport freight over 3,368 mi. (5,420 km) of track in Kentucky. Commercial airports with scheduled airline service are located at Louisville, Lexington, Owensboro, and Paducah. Border areas of the state are well served by the airports in Cincinnati, Ohio; Clarksville and Nashville, Tennessee; Evansville, Indiana; and Huntington, West Virginia.

SOCIAL AND CULTURAL LIFE

Museums: Kentucky has many museums specializing in local history. The Jean Thomas Museum in Ashland, the Appalachian Museum in Berea, and the Mountain Life Museum in London preserve important aspects of life in Kentucky's mountains. The Shaker Museum in South Union and Shaker Village at Pleasant Hill illustrate the way of life of a fascinating, and now nearly extinct, religious group. The Museum of History and Science in Louisville has exhibits pertaining to the history of the Ohio River Valley. The Filson Club Museum, also in Louisville, has books, manuscripts, and pioneer relics. The museum in Blue Licks Battlefield State Park, near Maysville, depicts the history of the area from the Ice Age through the period of the American Revolution. The Kentucky Museum in Bowling Green has collections relating to the state's cultural history, and Frankfort has both the Kentucky State Historical Museum and the Kentucky Military History Museum.

The spires
of Frankfort's
Paul Sawyer
Library and
Good Shepherd
Church

The J.B. Speed Art Museum, in Louisville, is the oldest and largest art museum in the state. Other art museums and galleries are in Augusta, Lexington, Owensboro, and Paducah. In Henderson, the John James Audubon Memorial Museum contains seven galleries with original Audubon paintings and many first-edition prints.

Natural history and archaeological exhibits are on display at the Behringer-Crawford Museum in Covington, the University of Kentucky Anthropology Museum in Lexington, and the Owensboro Area Natural Science Museum in Owensboro.

More-specialized museums are the Vent Haven Museum of Ventriloquism in Covington; Schmidt's Coca-Cola Museum in Elizabethtown; the Patton Museum of Cavalry and Armor in Fort Knox; and the Kentucky Derby Museum in Louisville.

Libraries: Kentucky state law requires that each county provide library services, either through the establishment of an independent library, by joining a regional library district, or by contracting with an existing library for services. All but eight of the counties have their own libraries; there are 173 libraries in the state. The Kentucky Department for Libraries and Archives, in Frankfort, provides many services to local libraries and librarians.

In addition to the local libraries, more than a hundred bookmobiles travel through the rural areas. The bookmobile idea is more than a hundred years old in Kentucky. It started with a "Traveling Book Project" in 1887. Books were shipped in wooden crates for loan to people in isolated areas. Later, mule-drawn and horse-drawn wagons were used. In 1937, Packhorse Libraries were organized. In each Packhorse Library, a librarian in charge organized the books and the service; four to six carriers rode horses or mules to deliver books and magazines to isolated mountain homes and schools.

Thoroughbred racing is a major spectator sport in Kentucky, especially on the first Saturday in May, when the Kentucky Derby is held at Churchill Downs.

Performing Arts: The people of Louisville take a lively interest in the performing arts, giving enthusiastic support to the Louisville Orchestra, the Kentucky Opera, the Louisville Ballet, the Broadway Series, and Stage One: Children's Theater, all of which put on regular performances at the striking, modern Kentucky Center for the Performing Arts. Various visiting artists give concerts at the lovely Louisville Palace, a renovated movie theater of the 1920s era. The Actors Theatre of Louisville has a fine and far-reaching reputation for excellence.

Lexington and Owensboro have local symphony orchestras, and a Festival of the Bluegrass is held each summer in Lexington. Ashland and Bowling Green have restored Art Deco movie theaters and use them as performing arts centers.

Outdoor dramatic performances are given each summer of *The Stephen Foster Story*, in Bardstown, and *The Legend of Daniel Boone* and *Lincoln*, in Harrodsburg. Other theaters are located in Danville, Horse Cave, Lexington, Paducah, and Prestonburg.

Sports and Recreation: Favorite spectator sports in Kentucky are college and high-school basketball, Louisville's minor-league baseball, and horse racing. In Lexington, Thoroughbred races are held at Keeneland Race Course, harness racing at the Red Mile Track, and many different events in which horses play a role at Kentucky Horse Park. Louisville has horse racing at Churchill Downs, including the Kentucky Derby on the first Saturday in May, and harness racing at Louisville Downs.

Water-related outdoor recreation is readily available throughout Kentucky. Hiking and climbing are popular in the mountains.

118

Historic Sites and Landmarks:

Ashland, in Lexington, was the home of Henry Clay. It was lived in by the Clay family for four generations and is furnished with original family possessions.

Blue Licks Battlefield in Mount Olivet was the location of the last battle of the revolutionary war. It was also a gathering spot for prehistoric animals.

Columbus-Belmont Battlefield State Park in Columbus was the site of a major skirmish early in the Civil War.

Constitution Square State Shrine in Danville is a reproduction of the state's first courthouse square, where Kentuckians met in 1784 to consider separation from Virginia. Kentucky's first state constitution was framed here.

Cumberland Gap National Historical Park marks the historic pass through the mountains used by the earliest pioneers coming into Kentucky. There is a visitor center and a restored mountain village.

Jefferson Davis Monument State Shrine in Fairview marks the birthplace of the president of the Confederate States of America with a 351-foot (107-meter) obelisk and a replica of the log cabin in which Davis was born.

Duncan Tavern Historic Shrine in Paris dates from 1788. Daniel Boone and other leading figures of his time often stopped here.

Fort Boonesborough, in Fort Boonesborough State Park south of Lexington, the site of Daniel Boone's settlement, is a reconstructed fort used as a museum and for craft demonstrations.

Fort Sequoyah, near London, is a restored village along Skagg's Trace, with a grist mill, a general store, a one-room schoolhouse, and other pioneer buildings.

Heritage Village, near Kentucky Dam, includes an Indian village, antique farm equipment, and an early log cabin.

Levi Jackson Wilderness Road State Park is in London, at the junction of the two famous pioneer trails into Kentucky: Boone's Trace and the Wilderness Road.

Abraham Lincoln Birthplace National Historic Site near Hodgenville is a 100-acre (40.5-hectare) site on which the log cabin believed to be the one in which Lincoln was born is enclosed inside a memorial building.

Lincoln Heritage House in Elizabethtown is a double log cabin that Thomas Lincoln, Abraham's father, helped to build. A one-room schoolhouse is also on the grounds.

Old Fort Harrod State Park in Harrodsburg features this reproduction of the original fort built two hundred years ago.

Lincoln Homestead State Park in Springfield was the home of Abraham Lincoln's forebears. The land was originally settled in 1782 by his grandfather. Several buildings have been reproduced.

Lincoln Marriage Temple in Harrodsburg is a building sheltering the log cabin in which Lincoln's parents were married. It was moved from its original site to the grounds of Old Fort Harrod State Park.

Mary Todd Lincoln House in Lexington was the girlhood home of the future First Lady.

McDowell House and Apothecary Shop in Danville is the restored home of the noted nineteenth-century surgeon Dr. Ephraim McDowell.

Old Cane Ridge Meeting House in Paris was built in 1791. It was the site of many revival meetings attracting tens of thousands of people during the Great Kentucky Revival, and was the birthplace of the Disciples of Christ (Christian Church).

Old Fort Harrod State Park in Harrodsburg features a reproduction of the original fort built two hundred years ago.

Old Mulkey Meeting House State Shrine in Tomkinsville is the oldest log meetinghouse in the state, dating from 1798.

Old Washington, south of Maysville, is a village that was founded in 1784. There are several restored cabins that date from the late 1700s and early 1800s.

Perryville Battlefield State Shrine in Perryville is the site of a major Civil War battle that involved more than six thousand troops.

Among the craft demonstrations carried out in Shaker Village at Pleasant Hill are spinning, wood crafting, and quilting.

Shaker Village at Pleasant Hill, near Harrodsburg, is a restored village built in the early 1800s. Craft demonstrations are carried out in several of the twenty-seven buildings. Early Shaker furniture is on display. There are overnight accommodations and restaurants.

Dr. Thomas Walker State Shrine at Barbourville contains a replica of the one-room log cabin he built near the river he named the Cumberland. Dr. Walker led the first known expedition through the Cumberland Gap, in 1750.

Waveland State Shrine in Lexington is a beautiful antebellum mansion and plantation village.

White Hall State Shrine in Richmond is the restored home of Cassius M. Clay, abolitionist, diplomat, and publisher of the antislavery paper *The True American*.

William Whitley House State Shrine in Stanford was one of the first brick houses constructed west of the Alleghenies.

Other Interesting Places to Visit

Ancient Buried City at Wickliffe is an archaeological site that was a city of the Mississippian mound-building culture about a thousand years ago. A museum interprets the findings.

Ballard County Wildlife Management Area near Wickliffe is a huge waterfowl refuge bordered by the Ohio River. There are eleven lakes on the acreage.

Big Bone Lick State Park near Walton has a museum and diorama exhibits that explain the prehistoric life that once inhabited the area.

Big South Fork Scenic Railway at Somerset offers two-hour rides through a rock tunnel and past abandoned coal camps. The railway operates only in the summer.

Bybee Pottery at Richmond dates from the early 1800s. Hand-thrown pottery is still being made by a fifth generation of the founding family.

Cathedral Basilica of the Assumption in Covington has one of the largest stained-glass windows in the world.

Empire Farm, at Land Between the Lakes, is a contemporary demonstration farm.

General Motors Assembly-Corvette Plant in Bowling Green conducts tours of the only Corvette assembly plant in the world.

The Homeplace-1850, in Aurora at Land Between the Lakes, is a living history farm.

Kentucky Horse Park, near Lexington, is a state park with two museums, facilities for many special events, and horse barns where a number of outstanding animals are kept on a temporary basis.

Kentucky State Capitol and other state buildings in Frankfort can be toured.

Kentucky Show in Louisville is a multimedia presentation of the state and its people.

Mammoth Cave National Park, northeast of Bowling Green, is the largest cave system in the world. The cave is open year-round, and the underground temperature stays at a constant 54 degrees Fahrenheit (12.2 degrees Celsius) all year. Several different tours are offered, including a boat trip on the underground Green River.

White Hall State Shrine in Richmond (above)
is the restored home of Cassius M. Clay—
abolitionist, diplomat, and publisher of
the antislavery paper *The True American*.
One of the caverns at Mammoth Cave
National Park features a formation called
the Ruins of Karnak (right).

Mammoth Onyx Cave near Horse Cave contains beautiful onyx formations in huge, high-ceilinged chambers. At the entrance to the cave is a wildlife area called Kentucky Buffalo Park.

My Old Kentucky Home State Park in Bardstown is the site of Federal Hill, the stately home that Stephen Foster visited frequently. The house, believed to be the place that inspired him to write the song, has early nineteenth-century furnishings, and attendants wear appropriate period costumes.

Natural Bridge State Park in Slade is a beautiful area of natural rock formations— arches, pinnacles, cliffs, and spires.

Old Harrodsburg Pottery in Harrodsburg has demonstrations of pottery making, candle dipping, and other crafts.

St. Joseph's Cathedral in Bardstown, built in 1819, contains several priceless paintings.

IMPORTANT DATES

13,000 B.C.-A.D. 900 — Prehistoric people live and hunt in Kentucky

900 — The mound-building Mississippian Culture flourishes

1669-1773 — Explorers make brief expeditions into Kentucky

1736 — French traders establish a village on the Ohio River, opposite the site of Portsmouth, Ohio

1750 — Dr. Thomas Walker leads an expedition into Kentucky through the Cumberland Gap for the Loyal Land Company

1751 — The Ohio Land Company sends Christopher Gist into northern Kentucky

1755 — Mary Inglis escapes from capture by the Shawnees and spends months wandering in the Kentucky wilderness

1767 — Daniel Boone first enters Kentucky

1773 — Falls of the Ohio (later named Louisville) is surveyed

1774 — First permanent white settlement is established, at Harrodsburg, by Virginian Colonel James Harrod

1775 — Settlements are established at Fort Boonesborough and other Kentucky locations

1776 — Kentucky officially becomes a county of the new state of Virginia

1778 — Settlers arrive at the Falls of the Ohio

1779 — Lexington is permanently settled, fort begun, and town laid out

1780 — Kentucky County is divided into three counties: Fayette, Jefferson, and Lincoln; town of Louisville is established at the Falls of the Ohio

1782 — Battle of Blue Licks, the last battle of the revolutionary war in the West

1783 — First horse race in Kentucky, at Humble's Race Path

1784 — First of ten conventions is called to discuss separation of Kentucky from Virginia

1786 — Frankfort is founded

1787—Kentucky's first newspaper, the *Kentucky Gazette,* begins publication

1792—Kentucky becomes the fifteenth state; first constitution is adopted; Isaac Shelby is inaugurated as first governor; capital is established at Frankfort; first post office west of the Allegheny Mountains is established at Danville

1798—The Kentucky Resolutions, sponsored by John Breckenridge, are passed, declaring the federal alien and sedition laws unconstitutional; Transylvania University is formed by union of Transylvania Seminary and Kentucky Academy

1799—Second Kentucky constitution is adopted; the Great Kentucky Revival begins

1803—Henry Clay is elected to United States House of Representatives, his first public office

1804—Disciples of Christ (Christian Church) is founded, near Paris

1805—A religious group known as the Shakers establishes a village at Pleasant Hill

1807—John J. Audubon arrives in Kentucky

1809—First successful operation for removal of an ovarian tumor is performed at Danville by Dr. Ephraim McDowell

1812—War of 1812 begins

1817—The first steamboat to go up the Mississippi and Ohio rivers from New Orleans reaches Louisville

1819—St. Joseph's Cathedral is built in Bardstown

1825—Marquis de LaFayette visits Kentucky

1832-35—Cholera epidemic causes many deaths in Kentucky

1833—Kentucky prohibits the importation of slaves except for those brought in by immigrants to the state

1835—First railroad service in the state is begun

1836—Kentuckian Richard M. Johnson elected vice-president of the United States

1846—War with Mexico begins; Kentuckian Zachary Taylor is appointed a major general

1848—Zachary Taylor is elected president of the United States; he dies in office in 1850

1849 — Third Kentucky constitution is written; it is adopted the following year

1853 — Stephen Foster publishes his song "My Old Kentucky Home"

1856 — Kentuckian John C. Breckinridge elected vice-president of the United States

1860 — Kentucky-born Abraham Lincoln is elected president of the United States

1861 — Civil War begins; Kentucky at first declares neutrality, later in the year joins the Union; a splinter state government is formed and joins the Confederate States of America

1863 — President Lincoln issues the Emancipation Proclamation

1865 — Civil War ends; President Lincoln is assassinated; Thirteenth Amendment to United States Constitution ends slavery in the United States

1875 — First Kentucky Derby is run, at Louisville's Churchill Downs; won by Aristides

1875-1905 — Period of infamous feuds in Kentucky

1887 — A Louisville woman initiates a "Traveling Book Project," forerunner of present-day bookmobiles that provide library services to isolated rural areas

1891 — Kentucky's fourth, and present, constitution is adopted

1896 — United States Supreme Court hands down Plessy Decision, establishing the principle of "separate but equal" facilities for blacks and whites

1898 — Spanish-American War

1900 — William Goebel is assassinated, but is declared governor before his death

1904 — Day Law is passed making integrated schools illegal

1905-07 — Tobacco War Night Riders are active in disputes over tobacco prices

1917-18 — America is involved in World War I

1920 — Nineteenth Amendment to United States Constitution gives women the right to vote

1922 — WHAS, first radio station in Kentucky, begins broadcasting

1925 — Frontier Nursing Service is founded to care for mountain women

1927-31 — A period of mine strikes and violent battles between strikers and strike breakers

1936—United States Treasury establishes gold depository at Fort Knox

1937—Great floods cause destruction along Ohio River and elsewhere

1941—Mammoth Cave estate becomes Mammoth Cave National Park

1941-45—America is involved in World War II

1946—Kentuckian Fred Vinson is selected chief justice of the United States

1949—Kentuckian Alben W. Barkley takes oath as vice-president of the United States

1950-53—America is involved in the Korean conflict

1954—United States Supreme Court declares segregated schools illegal; Kentucky integrates public schools peacefully

1955—Kentucky lowers legal voting age from twenty-one to eighteen

1966—Kentucky passes a strip-mine law to reclaim land destroyed by strip mining

1977—Kentucky passes antidiscrimination law, first southern state to do so

1978—Kentucky Horse Park opens near Lexington; a federal law goes into effect requiring strip-mine owners to reclaim land lost by surface mining

1983—Kentucky elects its first woman governor, Martha Layne Collins

1986—First Toyota plant in the United States begins construction near Georgetown

IMPORTANT PEOPLE

Muhammad Ali (1942-   ), born Cassius Marcellus Clay, Jr. in Louisville; Golden Gloves champion; Olympic medalist; first world champion heavyweight boxer to win the title four times

James Lane Allen (1849-1925), born near Lexington; author, novelist; used the Bluegrass as the setting for most of his books

Mary Anderson (1859-1940), noted actress; made her debut as Juliet in Louisville at age of sixteen; famous for her portrayal of Shakespearean and contemporary roles in the United States and England

MARY ANDERSON

127

JOHN J. AUDUBON

ROBERT W. BINGHAM

LOUIS D. BRANDEIS

SOPHONISBA BRECKINRIDGE

John James Audubon (1785-1851), famed naturalist and illustrator of North American birds; lived and painted in Kentucky from 1807 to 1820

Alben William Barkley (1877-1956), born in Graves County; politician; member United States House of Representatives (1913-27); United States senator (1927-49 and 1955-56); Democratic Senate majority leader (1937-47); vice-president of the United States (1949-53)

Robert Worth Bingham (1871-1937), newspaper publisher, diplomat; in 1918 bought control of *Louisville Courier-Journal* and *Louisville Times*; ambassador to Britain (1933-37)

Daniel Boone (1734-1820), frontiersman; hunted and explored in Kentucky in 1767 and from 1769-71; laid out the Wilderness Road through the Cumberland Gap to the Kentucky River in 1775; founded Boonesborough in 1775

Squire Boone (1744-1815), younger brother of Daniel, Indian fighter, explorer, Calvinist preacher

Louis Dembitz Brandeis (1856-1941), born in Louisville; lawyer, jurist, author; associate justice of the United States Supreme Court (1916-39); one of the first supporters of nature conservation; supporter of the Zionist movement to establish a Jewish state in Palestine

John Breckinridge (1760-1806), politician; attorney general of Kentucky (1795-97); United States senator (1801-05); United States attorney general (1805-06)

John Cabell Breckinridge (1821-1875), born near Lexington; vice-president of United States (1857-61), Civil War general; joined the Confederacy in 1861; brigadier general in Confederate army during the Civil War; Confederate secretary of war from February to April, 1965

Mary Breckinridge (1881-1965), founder in 1925 of the Frontier Nursing Service; dedicated her life to bringing health services to Kentuckians in isolated mountain areas; winner of several awards for public service

Sophonisba Preston Breckinridge (1866-1948), born in Lexington; lawyer, professor of social work, editor; at the University of Chicago in 1901 became the first woman to earn a Ph.D. in political science; was the first woman lawyer in Kentucky; leader in establishing standards for teaching social work; taught at the University of Chicago for thirty-eight years; in 1920 helped found the University of Chicago's School of Social Service Administration, which became the model for others in the nation

Simon Bolivar Buckner (1823-1914), born in Hart County; army officer, politician; lieutenant general in Confederate army during Civil War; governor of Kentucky (1887-91)

Christopher (Kit) Carson (1809-1868), born in Madison County; frontiersman, trapper, scout, Indian agent, Civil War brigadier general in the southwest

Albert B. ''Happy'' Chandler (1898-), born in Corydon; politician, baseball commissioner; governor of Kentucky (1935-39 and 1955-59); United States senator (1939-45); United States commissioner of baseball (1945-51)

George Rogers Clark (1752-1818), frontiersman, military leader, explorer; explored and surveyed Kentucky lands; his successful military strategies helped secure Kentucky and the Northwest for colonization

Cassius Marcellus Clay (1810-1903), born in Madison County; politician, emancipationist; in 1845 published abolitionist paper *The True American* in Lexington until mob violence forced its move to Cincinnati, Ohio; a founder of Republican party in 1854; United States minister to Russia (1861-62 and 1863-69)

Cassius Marcellus Clay, Jr. (see Muhammad Ali)

Henry Clay (1777-1852), statesman; moved to Lexington after passing the Virginia bar in 1797; member United States House of Representatives (1811-14, 1815-21, 1823-25); United States senator (1806-07, 1810-11, 1831-42, 1849-52); Speaker of the House of Representatives; campaigned for the presidency five times, unsuccessfully; known as the Great Compromiser and the Great Pacificator for his work on the Missouri Compromise, the Compromise of 1850, and other controversial issues

Irvin Shrewsbury Cobb (1876-1944), born in Paducah; journalist and humorist; author of books and plays

Floyd Collins (1887-1925), born in Barren County; cave explorer; discovered Crystal Cave in Mammoth Cave National Park in 1917; died while trapped in a nearby cave

Martha Layne Collins (1936-), born in Bagdad, Shelby County; first woman governor of Kentucky (1983-87)

John Sherman Cooper (1901-), born in Somerset; politician, diplomat; United States senator (1947-49, 1953-55, 1957-72); delegate to United Nations (1949-51); ambassador to India and Nepal (1955-56); ambassador to German Democratic Republic (1974-76); member of the Warren Commission that investigated the assassination of President John F. Kennedy

Jefferson Davis (1808-1889), born in Christian (now Todd) County; soldier, politician; member United States House of Representatives (1845-46); United States senator (1847-51 and 1857-61); secretary of war under President Franklin Pierce; first and only president of the Confederate States of America (1861-65)

Frank Duveneck (1848-1919), born Frank Decker in Covington; painter, sculptor, teacher

KIT CARSON

GEORGE ROGERS CLARK

HENRY CLAY

MARTHA LAYNE COLLINS

JOHN FILSON

ABRAHAM LINCOLN

LORETTA LYNN

THOMAS HUNT MORGAN

John Filson (1747?-1788), frontiersman, historian, educator; wrote *The Discovery, Settlement, and Present State of Kentucke,* a book that made Daniel Boone famous

John William Fox (1863-1919), born in Stony Point; novelist known as John Fox, Jr.; his books were set in the mountains of Kentucky; best-known novels are *The Little Shepherd of Kingdom Come* and *The Trail of the Lonesome Pine*

John Marshall Harlan (1833-1911) born in Boyle County; associate justice of the United States Supreme Court (1877-1911); best known for his dissenting opinions, especially for his dissent in the *Plessy vs. Ferguson* case of 1896, in which the Supreme Court sanctioned the "separate but equal" principle of racial segregation

James Harrod (1742-1793), frontiersman, surveyor, revolutionary war leader; founder in 1775 of Harrodsburg, the oldest permanent settlement in Kentucky; delegate to statehood conventions

Hatfields and McCoys, notorious feuding Appalachian families

Richard Mentor Johnson (1780-1850), born near Louisville; soldier, statesman; member of United States House of Representatives (1807-19 and 1829-37); United States senator (1819-29); vice-president of the United States (1837-41)

Abraham Lincoln (1809-1865), born in Hodgenville; sixteenth president of the United States (1861-65); member of United States House of Representatives (1847-49); in 1858, during an unsuccessful bid for United States Senate seat, engaged in famous debates with Stephen Douglas; in 1860 elected president of the United States; guided country through Civil War; in 1863 issued Emancipation Proclamation freeing slaves; assassinated by John Wilkes Booth five days after end of war

Mary Todd Lincoln (1818-1882), born in Lexington; wife of President Abraham Lincoln

Horace Harmon Lurton (1844-1914), born in Newport; jurist; associate justice of the United States Supreme Court (1910-14)

Loretta Lynn (1935-　　), born in Butcher Hollow; popular country music singer; creator of numerous gold albums; winner of 1971 Grammy award for "After the Fire is Gone"; in 1980 named entertainer of the decade (the 1970s) by the Academy of Country Music; autobiography *Coal Miner's Daughter* was made into a popular movie

Ephraim McDowell (1771-1830), surgeon; practiced in Danville; founder of modern abdominal surgery; performed first successful operation for removal of an ovarian tumor

Samuel Freeman Miller (1816-90), born in Richmond; jurist; associate justice of the United States Supreme Court (1862-90)

Thomas Hunt Morgan (1866-1945), born in Lexington; zoologist; recipient of the 1933 Nobel Prize in medicine for genetic research

Carry Amelia Moore Nation (1846-1911), born in Garrard County; crusader against evils of alcohol who went about the country destroying saloons; was arrested some thirty times for disturbing the peace

John Jacob Niles (1892-1980), born in Louisville; singer and composer, popularized many American folk ballads

Stanley Forman Reed (1884-1980), born in Maysville; jurist; associate justice of the United States Supreme Court (1938-57)

Alice Caldwell Hegan Rice (1870-1942), born in Shelbyville; novelist; best-known book is *Mrs. Wiggs of the Cabbage Patch*

Wiley Blount Rutledge (1894-1949), born in Cloverport; jurist; associate justice of the United States Supreme Court (1943-49)

Harland Sanders (1890-1980), businessman; from 1929 to 1956 ran a cafe in Corbin that specialized in fried chicken; came to be known as Colonel Sanders, the familiar Kentucky Colonel with white goatee and mustache who founded the worldwide chain of Kentucky Fried Chicken franchises

Isaac Shelby (1750-1826), first and fifth governor of Kentucky (1792-96 and 1812-16); revolutionary war hero; leader in War of 1812

Adlai Ewing Stevenson (1835-1914), born in Christian County; politician; vice-president of the United States (1893-97)

Barton Stone (1772-1844), clergyman; preacher at the Cane Ridge Church near Paris, which became the center for the Great Kentucky Revival; founder of Disciples of Christ (Christian Church); has been called "a kind of Johnny Appleseed" of early Christianity

Jesse Hilton Stuart (1907-1984), born near Riverton; author and educator; drew on his Kentucky mountain upbringing as inspiration for many of his poems, novels, and short stories

Zachary Taylor (1784-1850), twelfth president of the United States (1849-50); military leader; grew up near Louisville; served in War of 1812, the Black Hawk War, and the Mexican War; nicknamed "Old Rough and Ready"

Jean Bell Thomas (1881-1982), born in Ashland; writer and collector of Appalachian folk songs; known as the "Traipsin' Woman"; founder of the annual three-day American Folk Song Festival held each June in Ashland

Thomas Todd (1765-1826), jurist; chief justice of the Kentucky court system (1806); associate justice of the United States Supreme Court (1807-26)

Frederick Moore Vinson (1890-1953), born in Louisa; lawyer, jurist; member of United States House of Representatives (1923-29, 1931-38); secretary of the treasury (1945); chief justice of the United States Supreme Court (1946-53)

ALICE HEGAN RICE

WILEY B. RUTLEDGE

ISAAC SHELBY

ADLAI STEVENSON

WHITNEY M. YOUNG, JR.

Robert Penn Warren (1905-   ), born in Guthrie; novelist, poet, teacher, literary critic; received 1947 Pulitzer Prize in fiction for *All the King's Men*, the 1958 Pulitzer Prize in poetry for *Promises: Poems 1954-1956*, and the 1979 Pulitzer Prize in poetry for *Now and Then: Poems 1976-1978*; appointed first poet laureate of the United States (1986)

Henry Watterson (1840-1921), newspaper editor, politician; member of United States House of Representatives (1876-77); founder of Louisville *Courier-Journal*; received 1918 Pulitzer Prize for editorial writing

Whitney Moore Young, Jr. (1921-1971), born in Lincoln Ridge; civil-rights leader, social reformer, educator, author; dean of School of Social Work at Atlanta University (1954-61); executive director of National Urban League (1961-71); recipient of Medal of Freedom (1969)

GOVERNORS

Isaac Shelby	1792-1796	Simon B. Buckner	1887-1891
James Garrard	1796-1804	John Young Brown	1891-1895
Christopher Greenup	1804-1808	William O. Bradley	1895-1899
Charles Scott	1808-1812	William S. Taylor	1899-1900
Isaac Shelby	1812-1816	William Goebel	1900
George Madison	1816	J.C.W. Beckham	1900-1907
Gabriel Slaughter	1816-1820	Augustus E. Willson	1907-1911
John Adair	1820-1824	James B. McCreary	1911-1915
Joseph Desha	1824-1828	Augustus O. Stanley	1915-1919
Thomas Metcalfe	1828-1832	James D. Black	1919
John Breathitt	1832-1834	Edwin Porch Morrow	1919-1923
James T. Morehead	1834-1836	William J. Fields	1923-1927
James Clark	1836-1839	Flem D. Sampson	1927-1931
Charles A. Wickliffe	1839-1840	Ruby Laffoon	1931-1935
Robert P. Letcher	1840-1844	Albert B. Chandler	1935-1939
William Owsley	1844-1848	Keen Johnson	1939-1943
John Crittenden	1848-1850	Simeon S. Willis	1943-1947
John L. Helm	1850-1851	Earle C. Clements	1947-1950
Lazarus W. Powell	1851-1855	Lawrence W. Wetherby	1950-1955
Charles S. Morehead	1855-1859	Albert B. Chandler	1955-1959
Beriah Magoffin	1859-1862	Bert T. Combs	1959-1963
James R. Robinson	1862-1863	Edward T. Breathitt	1963-1967
Thomas E. Bramlette	1863-1867	Louie B. Nunn	1967-1971
John L. Helm	1867	Wendell H. Ford	1971-1974
John W. Stevenson	1867-1871	Julian M. Carroll	1974-1979
Preston H. Leslie	1871-1875	John Young Brown, Jr.	1979-1983
James B. McCreary	1875-1879	Martha Layne Collins	1983-1987
Luke P. Blackburn	1879-1883	Wallace Wilkinson	1987-
James Proctor Knott	1883-1887		

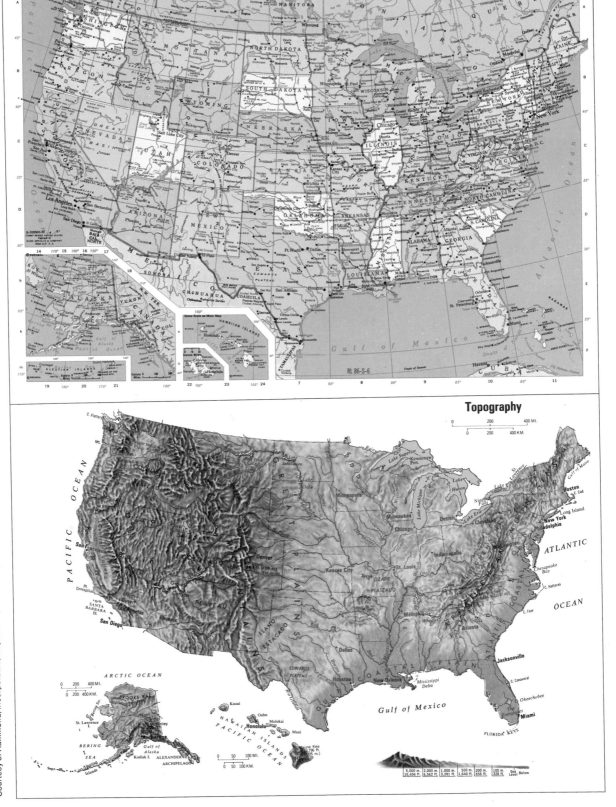

Topography

MAP KEY

Abraham Lincoln Birthplace National Historic Site	C4
Adairville	D3
Albany	D4
Alexandria	B5,k14
Allen	C7
Allensville	D2
Anchorage	g11
Arlington	f8
Ashland	B7
Auburn	D3
Augusta	B6
Barbourville	D6
Bardstown	C4
Bardwell	f8
Barkley Dam (dam)	C1,e9
Barlow	e8
Barren River (river)	C,D3
Barren River Lake (reservoir)	D3,4
Bayou de Chien (bayou)	f8,9
Bear Mountain (mountain)	C6
Beattyville	C6
Beaver Creek (creek)	C7
Beaver Dam	C3
Bedford	B4
Beech Fork (river)	C4
Bellevue	h14
Benham	D7
Benton	f9
Berea	C5
Berry	B5
Big Bone	k13
Big Sandy River (river)	B7
Black Mountain (mountain)	B,C7
Blaine Creek (creek)	B7
Bloomfield	C4
Bonnieville	C4
Booneville	C6
Bowling Green	C3
Bradfordsville	C4
Brandenburg	B4
Bremen	C3
Brodhead	C5
Brooks	g11
Brooksville	B6
Brownsboro	g12
Brownsville	C3
Buck Creek (creek)	C,D5
Buckhorn Lake (reservoir)	C6
Burgin	C5
Burkesville	D4
Burnside	D5
Butler	B5
Cadiz	C2,f10
Calhoun	C2
California	k14
Calvert City	e9
Campbellsburg	B4
Campbellsville	C4
Campton	C6
Caneyville	C3
Carlisle	B5
Carrollton	B4
Carrsville	C1,e9
Catlettsburg	B7
Cave City	C4
Cave Run Lake (lake)	B,C6
Centertown	C3
Central City	C2
Cerulean	f10
Chaplin River (river)	C4
Chimney Rock (mountain)	D5
Clarks River, West Fork (river)	f9
Clarkson	C3
Clay	C2,e10
Clay City	C6
Clearfield	B6
Clinton	f8
Clover Bottom	C5
Cloverport	C3
Cold Spring	h14
Columbia	D4
Columbus	f8
Corbin	D5
Corinth	B5
Corydon	C2
Crab Orchard	C5
Crescent Springs	h13
Crestwood	B4,g12
Crittenden	B5,k13
Crofton	C2
Cumberland	D7
Cumberland River (river)	D4
Cumberland Gap National Historic Park	D6
Cumberland Plateau (plateau)	C,D5,6,7
Dale Hollow Lake (lake)	D4
Danville	C5
Dawson Springs	C2
Dayton	B5,k14
Dewey Lake (reservoir)	C7
Dix River (river)	C5
Dix Dam (dam)	C5
Dixon	C2
Dover	A,B5
Drake Creek (creek)	D3
Drake Creek, West Fork (creek)	D3
Drakesboro	C3
Dry Ridge	B5
Dycusburg	C2
Eagle Creek (creek)	B5
Earlington	C2
Eddyville	C1,e9
Edgewood	h13
Edmonton	D4
Ekron	C3
Elizabethtown	C4
Elkhorn City	C7
Elkton	D2
Elsmere	h13
Eminence	B4
Erlanger	h13
Eubank	D5
Evarts	D6
Fairdale	g11
Fairfield	C4
Fairview	D2
Falmouth	B5
Falls of the Rough River	C3
Ferguson	D5
Fern Creek	g11
Fishtrap Lake (lake)	C7
Flag Knob (mountain)	C,D6
Flatwoods	B7

Flemingsburg	B6
Florence	B5,h13
Floyd Fork (river)	C4,g11,12
Fordsville	C3
Fort Knox	C4
Fort Thomas	B5,k14
Fort Wright	h13
Foster	B5,k14
Fountain Run	D4
Frankfort	B5
Franklin	D3
Fredonia	C1,e9
Frenchburg	C6
Frenchman Knob (peak)	C4
Fulton	e8
Gamaliel	D4
Georgetown	B5
Germantown	B6
Ghent	B4
Glasgow	D4
Glencoe	B5
Grand Rivers	e9
Grapevine	C2
Grayson Lake (lake)	B6,7
Greater Cincinnati Airport	h13
Green River (river)	C,D2,3
Green River Lake (lake)	C4
Greensburg	C4
Greenup	B7
Greenville	C2
Guist Creek (creek)	B4
Gunpowder Creek (creek)	k13
Guthrie	D2
Hanson	C2
Hardin	f9
Hardinsburg	C3
Harlan	D6
Harrods Creek (creek)	g11
Harrodsburg	C5
Hartford	C3
Hawesville	B3
Hazard	C6
Hazel	f9
Henderson	C2
Herrington Lake (lake)	C5
Hickman	f8
Hindman	C7
Hiseville	D4
Hodgenville	C4
Hopkinsville	D2
Horse Cave	C4
Hustonville	C5
Hyden	C6
Independence	B5,k13
Irvine	C6
Island	C2
Jackson	C6
Jamestown	D4
Jeffersontown	g11
Jeffersonville	C6
Jenkins	C7
Jeptha Knob (peak)	B4
Junction City	C5
Kentucky River (river)	B,C4,5
Kentucky River, Middle Fork (river)	C6,7
Kentucky River, North Fork (river)	C6,7
Kentucky River, South Fork (river)	C,D6
Kentucky Dam (dam)	e9
Kentucky Lake (lake)	e9,f9
Kentucky Ridge (mountain)	D6
Kevil	e9
Knob Creek (creek)	C4
Kuttawa	e9
La Center	e9
La Fayette	D2
La Grange	B4
Lake Barkley (lake)	e,f9,10
Lake Cumberland (lake)	D5
Lakeside Park	h13
Lancaster	C5
Land Between The Lakes	D1,e,f9
Laurel River Lake	C,D5,6
Lawrenceburg	C5
Lebanon	C4
Lebanon Junction	C4
Leitchfield	C3
Levisa Fork (river)	B,C7
Lewisburg	D2
Lewisport	B3
Lexington	C5
Liberty	C5
Licking River (river)	B,C5,6,k14
Licking River, North Fork (river)	B,C6
Licking River, South Fork (river)	B6
Little River (river)	D2
Little Sandy River (river)	B6,7
Livermore	C2
Livingston	C5
Lockport	B5
London	D5
Loretto	C4
Louisa	B7
Louisville	B4,g11
Loyall	D6
Ludlow	h13
Lynch	D7
Lyndon	g11
Mackville	C4
Madisonville	C2
Mammoth Cave National Park	C4
Manchester	D6
Marion	C1,e9
Markland Lock Dam	B5
Martin	C7
Mayfield	f9
Maysville	B6
McAlpine Lock & Dam	g11
McHenry	C3
McKee	C6
McRoberts	C7
Melbourne	h14
Mentor	k14
Middlesboro	D6
Middletown	g11
Midway	B5
Millersburg	B5
Milton	B4
Mississippi River (river)	C,D1,e,f,g,h8,9
Monterey	B5
Monticello	D5
Morehead	B6
Morganfield	C2
Morgantown	C3
Mortons Gap	C2
Mount Olivet	B6
Mount Olympus (mountain)	C6
Mount Sterling	B6
Mount Vernon	C5
Mount Washington	C4
Mountain Ash	D5
Mud River (river)	C3
Mud Lick Creek (creek)	k13
Muldraugh	C4
Munfordville	C4
Murray	f9
Nebo	C2
Neon	C7
New Castle	B4
New Haven	C4
Newport	A5,h14
Nicholasville	C5
Nolin River (river)	C3,4
Nolin Lake (lake)	C3
North Corbin	D5
North Middletown	B5
Nortonville	C2
Oak Grove	D2
Oakland	C3
Ohio River (river)	C1,2,3,B3,4,5,A5,B5,6,7, e8,9,10,g11,12,h,k13,14
Okolona	g11
Olive Hill	B6
Owensboro	C2
Owenton	B5
Owingsville	B6
Paducah	e9
Paintsville	C7
Paris	B5
Park City	C3
Park Hills	h13
Peach Orchard Knob (peak)	D2
Pembroke	D2
Perryville	C5
Pewee Valley	B4,g12
Persimmon Grove	k14
Phelps	C7
Pikeville	C7
Pine Knot	D5
Pine Mountain (range)	C,D6,7
Pineville	D6
Pleasure Ridge Park	g11
Pleasureville	B4
Pond Creek (creek)	g11
Pond River (river)	C2
Pond River, West Fork (river)	C2,3
Poplar Mountain (mountain)	C,D7
Prestonburg	C7
Prestonville	B4
Princeton	C2
Prospect	g11
Providence	C2,e10
Rabbit Hash	g10
Raceland	B7
Radcliff	C4

Ravenna	C6
Red River (river)	C6
Red Bird Creek (creek)	C6
Reidland	e9
Richmond	C5
Rochester	C3
Rockcastle River (river)	C,D5
Rockport	C3
Rolling Fork (river)	C4
Rough River (river)	C3
Rough River Lake (lake)	C3
Russell	B7
Russell Fork (river)	C7
Russell Springs	C4
Russellville	D3
Sacramento	C2
Sadieville	B5
St. Charles	C2
St. Matthews	g11
Salem	C1,e9
Salt Lick	B6
Salt River (river)	B,C4,5,g11,12
Salyersville	C7
Sanders	B5
Sandy Hook	B7
Sardis	B6
Science Hill	D5
Scottsville	D3
Sebree	C2
Sharpsburg	B6
Shelbyville	B4
Sheperdsville	C4
Shively	g11
Silver Grove	k14
Sinking Creek (creek)	C3
Slaughters	C2
Smithland	e9
Smiths Grove	C3
Somerset	D5
Sonora	C4
South Williamson	C7
Southgate	h14
Sparta	B5
Springfield	C4
Stamping Ground	B5
Stanford	C5
Stanton	C6
Stearns	D5
Stringtown	C5
Sturgis	C2,e10
Taylor Mill	h13
Taylorsville	C4
Tennessee River (river)	A5,h14
Tollesboro	B6
Tompkinsville	D4
Tradewater River (river)	C,D2,e10
Tug Fork (river)	B,C7
Tygarts Creek (creek)	B6,7
Union	B5,k13
Uniontown	C1,e10
Upton	C4
Valley Station	g11
Vanceburg	B6
Van Lear	C7
Verda	D6
Versailles	C5
Vicco	C6
Vine Grove	C4
Visalia	k14
Walton	B5,k13
Warsaw	B4
Washington	B6
Water Valley	f9
Waverly	C2
Wayland	C7
West Liberty	C6
West Point	C4
Westwood	B7
Wheatcroft	C2,e10
Wheelwright	C7
White Plains	C2
White Rocks (mountain)	D6
Whitesburg	C7
Whitesville	C2
Whitley City	D5
Wickliffe	f8
Williamsburg	D5
Williamstown	B5
Willisburg	C4
Wilmore	C5
Winchester	C5
Wingo	f9
Woodburn	D3
Woodlawn	g10
Wooler Creek (creek)	k13
Worthington	B7
Zebulon	C7

OHIO

INDIANA

KENTUCKY

Cincinnati

Louisville

Lexington

Huntington

Ashland

Portsmouth

Ironton

Evansville

Bowling Green

Dayton

Springfield

Hamilton

Middletown

Carbondale

Cape Girardeau

New Madrid

Clarksville

MAMMOTH CAVE NAT'L PARK

LAND BETWEEN THE LAKES RECREATION AREA

Kentucky Lake

Lake Barkley

Lake Cumberland

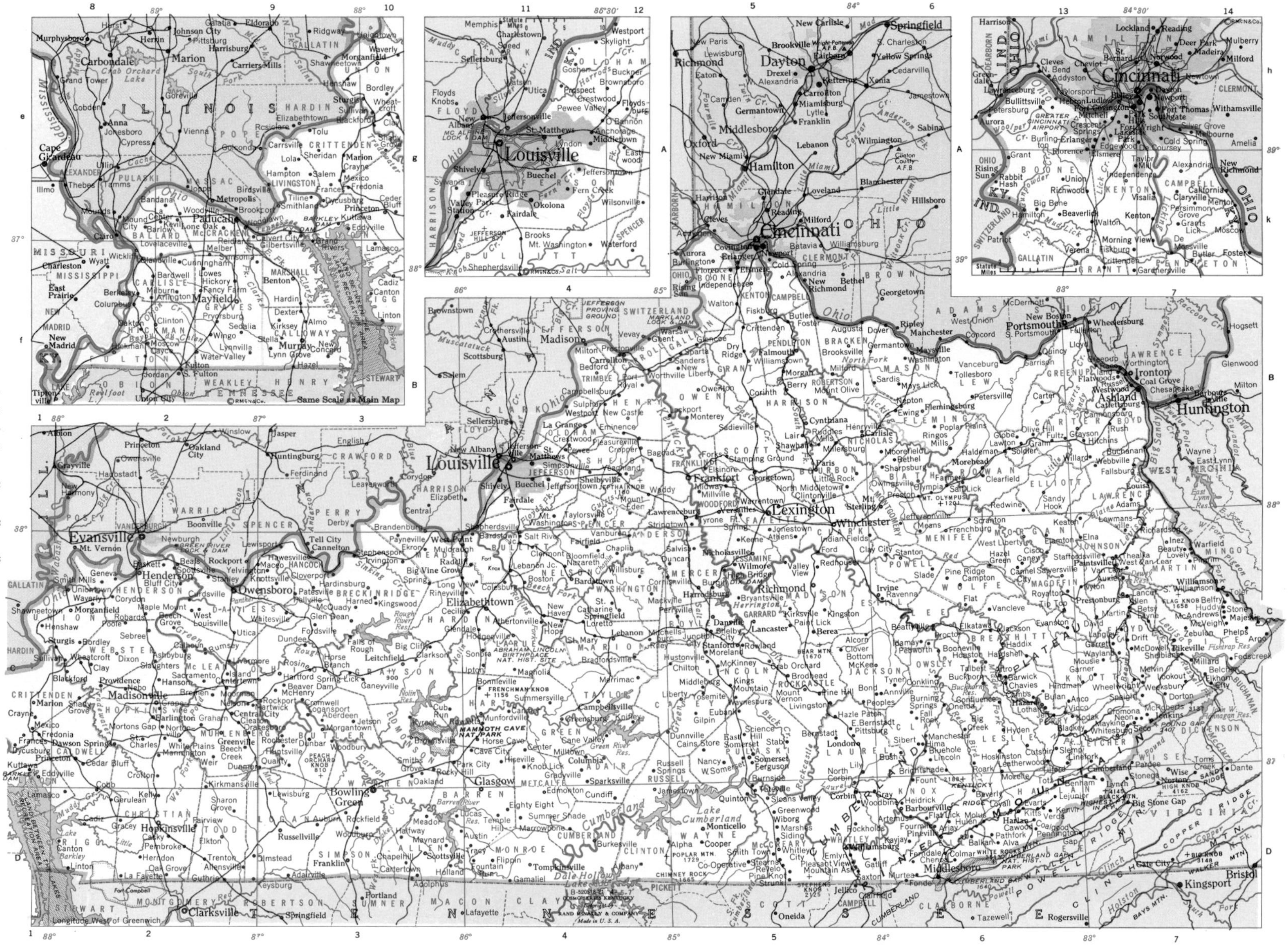

Statute Miles 5 0 10 20 30 40

Kilometers 5 0 5 10 20 30 40 50 60

Lambert Conformal Conic Projection

Same Scale as Main Map

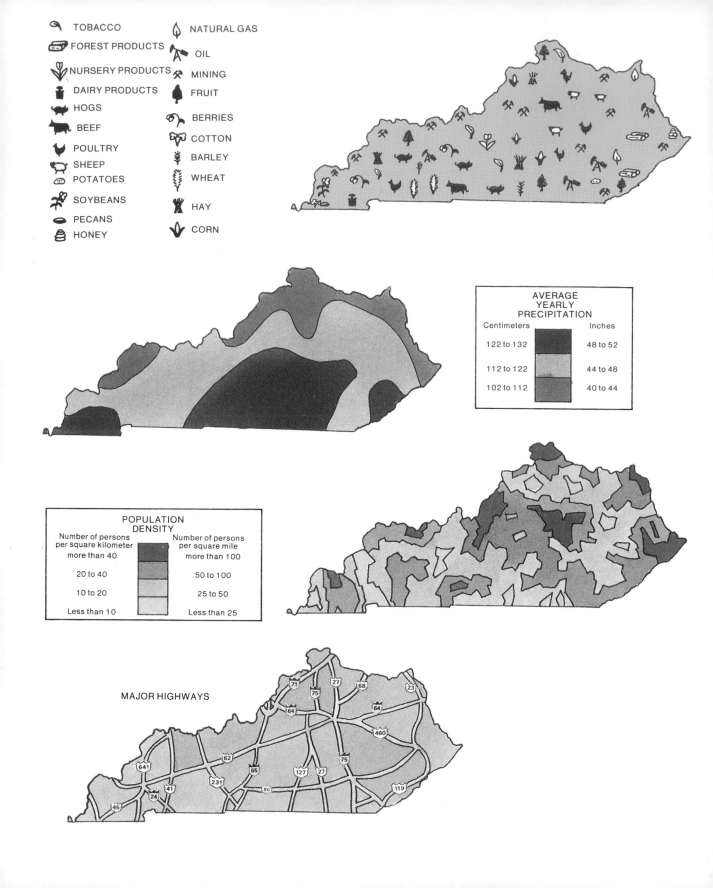

TOBACCO
FOREST PRODUCTS
NURSERY PRODUCTS
DAIRY PRODUCTS
HOGS
BEEF
POULTRY
SHEEP
POTATOES
SOYBEANS
PECANS
HONEY
NATURAL GAS
OIL
MINING
FRUIT
BERRIES
COTTON
BARLEY
WHEAT
HAY
CORN

AVERAGE
YEARLY
PRECIPITATION

Centimeters		Inches
122 to 132		48 to 52
112 to 122		44 to 48
102 to 112		40 to 44

POPULATION
DENSITY

Number of persons per square kilometer		Number of persons per square mile
more than 40		more than 100
20 to 40		50 to 100
10 to 20		25 to 50
Less than 10		Less than 25

MAJOR HIGHWAYS

TOPOGRAPHY

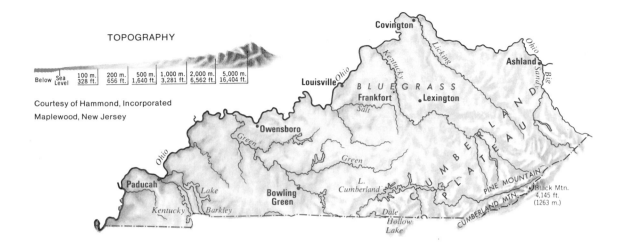

| Below Sea Level | 100 m. 328 ft. | 200 m. 656 ft. | 500 m. 1,640 ft. | 1,000 m. 3,281 ft. | 2,000 m. 6,562 ft. | 5,000 m. 16,404 ft. |

Courtesy of Hammond, Incorporated

Maplewood, New Jersey

COUNTIES

Autumn color, Lake Cumberland

INDEX

Page numbers that appear in boldface type indicate illustrations

abolitionists, 40-42
Actors Theatre of Louisville, 84
Adams, John Quincy, 34
agriculture, 14, 15, 34-35, 70-71, 115
airlines, 57
airports, 57, 69, 116
Allen, James Lane, 127
All the King's Men, 86
American Association, 51
American Colonization Society, 41

American Revolution, 31, 97
American Saddle Horse, 79
American Saddle Horse Museum, 99
Anderson, Mary, 127, **127**
animal, state, **108**, 109
animals, 18-19, 96, 113
Appalachian Mountains, 28, 102
Appalachian Plateau, 10
area, of state, 112
Arnow, Harriet, 86
Arthur, Gabriel, 28

Ashland, 101
Audubon, John James, 106, 128, **128**
auger mining, 14, 72-73
Australian ballot, 66
automobiles, 51, 57
Back Home in Kentucky, 69
banjo, 82
Baptists, 24, 36, 41
Bardstown, 25, 37, **37**, 85, 95
Barkley, Alben William, 58-59, 128

Barren River, 15
baseball, 51, 60, 89, 118
basketball, 88, 118
Bat Cave, 101
Batts, Thomas, 28
Belle of Louisville, 92
Berea, 67, 68, 83, 101, 104
Berea College, 47, 67-68, 74, 101
Bernheim Forest Arboretum and
    Nature Center, 95
Big Bone Lick State Park, 96
Big Sandy River, 102
bill of rights, 31-32, 65
Bingham, Robert Worth, 128, **128**
bird, state, **108**, 109
birds, 15, 19, 100, 106, 113
Birds of America, The, 106
Birney, James G., 41
Birth of a Nation, 86
blacks, 23, 24, 40-42, 44, **44**, 45,
    45-46, 46-47, 60-61, 66-67, **67**
"Bloody Harlan County," 56
bluegrass, 12
Bluegrass, 10, 12-13, 70, 76, 77,
    82, 98-101
Bluegrass Magazine, 69
bluegrass music, 82
Bluegrass State Games, 89
Blue Licks, 30
Blue Licks Battlefield State Park,
    97
boating, 15, 16, 106
Boone, Daniel, 29, 76, 97, 101,
    102, 105, 128
Boone, Squire, 29, 128
Boonesborough, 29, 30
Boone Tavern Hotel, 68
borders, of state, 11, 112
Bowling Green, 13, 60, 69, 105
Brady, Matthew, **43**
Brandies, Louis Dembitz, 128,
    128
Breaks of the Mountains, 102
Breathitt, Edward, 61
Breckinridge, John, 128
Breckinridge, John Cabell, 128
Breckinridge, Mary, 128
Breckinridge, Sophonisba
    Preston, 128, **128**
Broadway Series, 84

Buckley Wildlife Sanctuary, 100
Buckner, Simon Bolivar, 128
California, 23
Calumet Farm, 99
camping, 106
canals, 34
capitals, state, 32, 100, 101, 109
Cardinals, 88
Carolinas, 40
Carrollton, 83
Carson, Christopher (Kit), 129,
    129
Carter, Jimmy, 25
Carter Caves State Resort Park,
    101
Cascade Caves, 101
Cathedral Basilica of the
    Assumption, **96**
Caudill, Harry M., 86
Caudill, Rebecca, 86
Cave, The, 86
Cavelier, René-Robert, 28
caves, 14, 16-18, **17**, 105
Chandler, Albert B. "Happy,"
    58, **58**, 129
Cherokees, 27
Chicago, 60
Chickasaw Indians, 14, 27
chronology, 124-127
Churchill Downs, **4**, 79, 89, 92,
    118
Cincinnati, Ohio, 57, 60, 96-97,
    97
Cincinnati Reds, 60, 89
civil rights, 44, 44-45, 47, 60-61
Civil Rights Movement, 60-61
Civil War, 7, 22, 25, 34, 36,
    38-39, 41, 42-44, **43-44**, 47, 48,
    49, 64, 65, 85, 101, 106
Clark, George Rogers, 129, **129**
Clay, Cassius M., 41, **41**, **123**, 129
Clay, Henry (Great
    Compromiser), **33**, 33-34,
    40-41, 98, 129, **129**
Clermont, 95
climate, 18, 113
coal mining, 11, 14, 35, 49, 53,
    54-56, **55**, 59, 71-73, **72**, 115
Cobb, Irving Shewsbury, 87, 129
Coca-Cola Museum, 93-94

colleges, 35, 36, 67-68, 115
Collins, Floyd, 129
Collins, Martha Layne, 66, 129,
    129
Colonel Harland Sanders
    Museum, 93
Columbus-Belmont Battlefield,
    106
communication, 69-70, 115
company towns, 54
Confederate States of America,
    42, 107
constitutions, state, 31-32, 65-67
Cooper, John Sherman, 129
Corbin, 104, 105
counties, number of, 63-65, 114,
    137 (map of)
courts, 63-65, 66, 114
Covington, 69, 96-97, **96-97**
crafts, **5**, 74, **87**, 87-88, **121**
crops, 71
Crystal Onyx Cave, 105
cultural life, 82-88, 116-123
Cumberland Falls, **104**, 104-105
Cumberland Gap, 28, 105
Cumberland Lake, 16, **138**
Cumberland Mountains, 11
Cumberland Plateau, 10
Cumberland River, 15, 16, **112**
Cumberland River Gorge, 105
Dale Hollow Lake, 16
dams, 16, **16**
Daniel Boone National Forest,
    103
Danville, 32, 35, 84 101
"Dark as a Dungeon," 55
Davis, Jefferson, 42, **43**, 107, 129
Day Law, 67
Delaware, 43
Democratic party, 25, 44
Detroit, 60
Diamond Caverns, **17**, 105
Disciples of Christ, 24, 36, 37
distances, greatest, 112
Dixie Belle Riverboat, 100
dulcimer, 82, **83**
Duveneck, Frank, 129
Eastern Coal Field, 10, 11
Eastern Kentucky University, 67
economy, 49, 59, 60, 70, 115-116

education, 35-36, 46-47, 52, 56, 60, 66-68, **67-68**, 115
Elizabethtown, 93-94
Emancipation Proclamation, 43
English, in Kentucky, 22, 28-29
Episcopalians, 24
European explorers, hunters, 28-29
Evansville, 60
Exit Laughing, 87
Fairview, 107
Fallam, Robert, 28
Falls of Ohio, 13, 34
Falmouth, 97
farming, 11, 14, 15, 34, 49, 51, 70-71, **71**
Festival of the Bluegrass, 84
Fifteenth Amendment, 45
Filson, John, 130, **130**
fish, 19, 73, 113
fish, state, 109
fishing, 15, 105, 106
flag, state, **108**, 109
flower, state, **108**, 109
folk arts, 74, 102
forests, 10, 12, 16, 19, 73
Fort Boonesborough, **30**
Fort Boonesborough State Park, 101
Fort Knox, 57, **57**, 93
Fort Mitchell, 96
Foster, Stephen, 85, **85**, 95, 110
Founders Square, 92
Fourteenth Amendment, 45
Fox, John William, Jr., 86, 130
Frankfort, 32, 52, 61, 89, 100
Free Soil party, 41
French, in Kentucky, 22, 24, 28
Fugitive Slave Law, 44, **44**
geography, 10-11, 112-113
Georgetown, 89
Germans, in Kentucky, 22, 24
Giles, Janice Holt, 86
Gist, Christopher, 29
gold reserves, 57
Good Shepherd Church, **117**
government, 31, 32, 63-66, 70, 73, 114
governor's mansion, **64**
governors, list of, 132

Great Compromise of 1850, 34
Great Depression (1930s), 56-57
Great Ohio River Flatboat Race, 106
Great Saltpeter Cave, 104
Green River, 15
Griffith, David W., 86
Harlan, Justice John Marshall, **47**, 130
harness racing, 78-79, 89
Harrington Lake, 16
Harrod, James, 130
Harrodsburg, 29, 85, 100
Hatfields, 48, **48**, 103, 130
Henderson, 14, 106
Henderson, Richard, **31**
highest point, 11, 112
highways, 15, 57, 68-69, **69**, 116
highways, major, map of, **136**
hiking, 103, 106, 118
historic sites and landmarks, 119-123
Hodgenville, 94
Horse Cave, 84
horse farms, 12-13, 77, **77**
horse racing, 78, **78**, 79, 89, 118, **118**
house of representatives, state, 66, 114
Hundred Dome Cave, 105
hunters, 28
Huntington, West Virginia, 69
improvers' cabins, 29
Indianapolis, 57
integration, 67, **67**
International Museum of the Horse, 99
Irish, in Kentucky, 22
Iroquois League (Five Nations), 27
Jackson, Andrew, 14
Jackson Purchase, 11, 14-15
Jean Thomas Museum and Cultural Center, 102
Jefferson, Thomas, 32
Jenny Wiley State Park, **102**
Jesse James Cave, 105
Jockey Club, 78
John James Audubon State Park, 106

Johnson, Richard Mentor, 130
Jolliet, Louis, 28
Keeneland Race Course, 89, 98
Kentucky
   origin of name, 27-28, 109
   six geographic regions of, 10-15
Kentucky Center for the Performing Arts, 84
Kentucky Derby, **78**, 79, 118, **118**
Kentucky Derby Museum, 92
Kentucky Highlands Museum, 102
Kentucky Horse Park, 98-99, **99**
Kentucky Lake, 15, 16, 106, **107**
Kentucky Opera, 84
Kentucky Railway Museum, 93
Kentucky Revival era, **36**, 36-37
Kentucky River, 15, 100
Kentucky Scottish Weekend, 83
Kentucky State Historical Museum, **116**
Kentucky Wesleyan, 89
KET, television station, 70, 115
King, Martin Luther, Jr., 61
Knobs, 10, 13
Ku Klux Klan (KKK), 45-46
labor unions, 56
Lake Barkley, 15, 16, 106, 107
lakes, 15-16, **16**, 113
Land Between the Lakes, 15, 106
La Salle, René-Robert Cavelier, Sieur de, 28
Laurel River Lake, **16**
legislature, state, 31, **31**, 32, 42, 52, 64, 66, 114
Levi Jackson State Park, 104
Lexington, 12, 13, 24, 30, 35, **35**, 41, 60, 67, 69, 83, 84, 88, 89, 98, **98**, 100, 101, **110**
Lexington Herald-Leader, 69
Liberia, 41, **41**
Liberty party, 41
libraries, 117, **117**
Licking River, 15
Lincoln, Abraham, 42, 43, **43**, 44, **94**, 94-95, 101, 130, **130**
Lincoln, Mary Todd, 130
Lincoln, Thomas, 101
Lincoln, 85

The Kentucky long-rifle team participates in the Derby Festival Parade.

Lincoln Heritage House, 94
Lincoln Jamboree, 95
Lindbergh,Charles, 57
liquor industry, 58, 74
literature, 86-87
Little Shepherd of Kingdom Come, The, 86
Livingston, 104
logging, 11
Louisiana Purchase, 32
Louisville, 12, **12**, 13, 24, 30, **35**, 49, 51, 52, **52**, 57, 60, **61**, 66, 67, **67**, 69, 79, 84, 89, 92-93, **93**, 96
Louisville Ballet, 84
Louisville Courier-Journal, 69
Louisville Orchestra, 84
Louisville Palace, 84
Louisville Slugger bats, 51
lowest point, 112
lowlands, 15
Loyal Land Company, 28
Lurton, Horace Harmon, 130
Lutherans, 24
Lynn, Loretta, 130, **130**
Madisonville, 14
magazines, 69
Maine, 34
Main Strasse Village, 97

Mammoth Cave, 14, 18, 105
Mammoth Cave National Park, **17**, 122, **123**
manufacturing, 14, 35, 70, 73, 115
maps, of Kentucky
  counties, **137**
  highways, major, **136**
  political, **135**
  population density, **136**
  precipitation, **136**
  products, principal, **136**
  topographical, **137**
maps, of United States
  political, **133**
  topographical, **133**
Marquette, Father Jacques, 28
marshlands, 19
Masterson Station Park, 84
Maysville, 30
McCoys, 48, 103, 130
McDowell, Ephraim, 130
Methodists, 24, 36, 37, 41
Midway, 100
Miller, Samuel Freeman, 130
minerals and mining, 35, 115
Mingo County, West Virginia, 48

Mississippi Plateau, 11
Mississippi River, 15, 28, 32, 106
Mississippian Sea, 16
Missouri, 34
Missouri Compromise of 1820, 34
Monroe, Bill, 82
Montgomery, Alabama, 42, 47
Morgan, Thomas Hunt, 130
motto, state, 109
Mountain Life Museum, 104
mountain music, 82-83, **83**
Mrs. Wiggs of the Cabbage Patch, 87
Muhammad Ali, 127
museums, 116-117
"My Old Kentucky Home," 7, 85, **85**, 95, 110
My Old Kentucky Home State Park, 95
Nashville, 60
Nation, Carry Amelia Moore, 131
National Audubon Society, 100
Natural Bridge, 103
Natural Bridge State Park, 103, **103**
New Orleans, 34

newspapers, 69, 115
nickname, state, 12, 109
Night Riders, 53
Niles, John Jacob, 131
Ohio Land Company, 29
Ohio River, 10, 12, 13, 14, 15, 19, 22, 27, 28, **30**, 92, 96, 102, 106
Ohio Valley, 28
Old Fort Harrod, 100
Old Fort Harrod State Park, **120**
Olive Hill, 83
Owensboro, 14, 24, 60, 89, 106
Paducah, 15, 60
Parks, Rosa, 47
Patton Museum of Cavalry and Armor, 93
Paul Sawyer Library, **117**
Pennyroyal (Pennyrile), 10, 13-14
people, of Kentucky, **20-21**, 22-25, **23**
people, of Kentucky, important, 127-132
performing arts, 82-86, 118
Perryville Battlefield State Shrine, 101
Pike County, Kentucky, 48
Pine Mountains, 11
Pioneer Playhouse, 84
pioneers, 29-31, **29**, **30**
Pittsburgh, 34
plants, 19, 113
Pleasant Hill, 37, **37**, 100
Plessy, Homer, 47
poet laureate, United States, 86
politics, 25
population figures, 24, 31, 35, 49, 60, 111
precipitation, 18, 113, **136** (map of)
prehistory, 27-28
Presbyterian Kentucky Academy, 35
Presbyterians, 24, 36, 37, 41
products, principal, 74, 115, **136** (map of)
Public Works Administration (PWA), 56
radio, 57
radio stations, 69

railroads, 15, 34, 49, 51, 69, 116
Reconstruction era, 44-45
recreation, 15, 16, 95, 100-101, 103-106, 108
Redbirds, 89
Red Mile Track, 98
Red River Gorge Geological Area, 103
Reed, Stanley Forman, 131
religion, 24-25, 36-37, **36-37**
Renfro Valley, 83, 104
Renfro Valley Barn Dance, 83
Renfro Valley Country Music Center, 104
Republican party, 25
Rice, Alice Caldwell Hegan, 86-87, 131, **131**
Richmond, Virginia, 89
rivers, 15-16, 113
Roberts, Elizabeth Madox, 86
Roman Catholics, 25, 37
Romance of Billy Goat Hill, A, 87
Roosevelt, Franklin D., 56
Rough River Dam State Resort Park, 95
Rough River Lake, 95
Rural Kentuckian, 69
rural life, 51-52
Rutledge, Wiley Blount, 131, **131**
Salley, John Peter, 28
salt licks, 96, 97
Salt River, 15
Sanders, Harland, 131
schools, 35-36, 46-47, 52, 60, 66-67, **67**, 115
Scottish, in Kentucky, 22
segregation, 47, 66-67
senate, state, 66, 114
"separate but equal" ruling, 47, **47**
service industries, 70, 73
Shakers, 37, **37**, 85, 88
Shakertown Revisited, 85
Shaker Village, 37, **121**
Shawnees, 27
Shelby, Isaac, 131, **131**
shipping, 34, 92
"Sixteen Tons," 54
slavery, 32, 34, 40-42, 43, 45, 65
social life, 116-118

soil erosion, 14, 53, 73
song, state, 7, 110
Spanish, in Kentucky, 24
Spirit of St. Louis, 57
sports, 88-89, 118, **118**
Springfield, 101
St. Joseph's Cathedral, 37, **37**, 95
Stage One: Children's Theater, 84
Standardbred horses, **78**, 78-79
statehood, 31, 109
state parks, 15, 95
Stephen Foster Story, The, 95
Stevenson, Adlai Ewing, 131, **131**
Stone, Barton, 131
Stone Castle Museum, 95
strip mining, 14, 53, 72-73, **72**
Stuart, Jesse Hilton, 86, 101-102, 131
Supreme Court, 47, **47**, 67
swamps, 15, 96
swimming, 15, 106
taxes, 58
Taylor, Zachary, 131
television stations, 70, 115
temperature, 18, 113
Tennessee, 40, 105
Tennessee River, 15, 16
Tennessee Valley Authority (TVA), 16
Texas, 23
Thirteenth Amendment, 43, 45
Thomas, Jean Bell, 131
Thomas, Opera House, 84
Thoroughbred horses, 12, 70, 75, 76-79, **77-78**
tobacco industry, 13, 15, 49, **49**, 52-53, 58, 70, **71**
Tobacco War, 52-53
Todd, Mary, 98
Todd, Thomas, 131
topography, 113, **133**, (U. S. map), **137** (Kentucky map)
tourism, 15, 68, 92-107
Tradewater River, 15
Trail of the Lonesome Pine, The, 86
transportation, 13, 34, 51, 68-69, **69**, 116

Transylvania Academy, 35
Transylvania Land Company, 29
Transylvania Seminary, 35
Transylvania University, 35, 67, **68**
Travis, Merle, 54, 55
tree, state, **108**, 109
trees, 10, 12, 16, 19, 73, 113
True American, The, 41
Truman, Harry S., 59
underground mining, 14
unemployment rate, 70
United Mine Workers, 25, 56
universities, 67-68, 115
University of Kentucky, 67, **68**, 88

University of Louisville, 36, 67, 88
Vent Haven Museum, 96
Vinson, Frederick Moore, 131
Virginia, 31, 40, 101, 105
voting rights, 45, 66
Wagner Labor Relations Act, 56
Walker, Thomas, 28, 105
War of 1812, 33, 35, 64
Warren, Robert Penn, 86, 132
water pollution, 14, 54, 73
water skiing, 15
water sports, 15, 118
waterways, 34, 69, 116
Watterson, Henry, 132
Weisenberger Mill, 100, **100**
Western Coal Field, 11, 14

Western Kentucky University, 67
White Hall State Shrine, **123**
Wickliffe, 106
Wilderness Road, 29
wildflowers, 19, **19**, 113
wild plants, 19, **19**, 113
Wiley, Jenny, 102-103
Willson, Augustus E., 53
Wood, Abram, 28
Works Progress Administration (WPA), 56
World Enough and Time, 86
World War I, 53-54, 55
World War II, 59, 82
Young, Whitney Moore, Jr., 132, **132**

Picture Identifications

Front cover: Horse farm in the Bluegrass region
Back cover: Breaks of the Sandy in the Cumberland Mountains
Pages 2-3: Cumberland Gap
Page 6: ''My Old Kentucky Home'' in Bardstown
Pages 8-9: The Appalachian foothills
Pages 20-21: Montage of Kentuckians
Page 27: Painting of Daniel Boone on the Wilderness Road
Pages 38-39: The Battle of Mill Spring
Page 50: Knott County farmer Cody Jacobs plowing his field
Page 62: The Capitol, Frankfort
Page 75: A jockey being led to the starting gate at Churchill Downs on Derby Day
Pages 80-81: The riverboat *Belle of Louisville*
Page 81 (inset): Kentucky Center for the Performing Arts, Louisville
Pages 90-91: Red River Gorge in Daniel Boone National Forest, Cumberland Mountains
Page 90 (inset): Louisville night scene
Page 108: Montage showing the state flag, the state bird (Kentucky cardinal), the state tree (Kentucky coffee tree), the state animal (gray squirrel), and the state flower (goldenrod)

Picture Acknowledgments

H. Armstrong Roberts: © F. Ross: Front cover; © R. Krubner: Pages 4, 61; © Camerique: Pages 12, 93; © C.S. Bauer: Page 71 (left)
© **W. Ray Scott:** Back cover, pages 5, 11, 16, 17 (both pictures), 20 (top right), 21 (top right), 30 (right), 64, 68 (both pictures), 69, 71 (right), 78 (both pictures), 85 (right), 87 (top left and right), 90-91, 94 (left), 96, 97, 99, 100, 102 (both pictures), 103, 107, 108 (bottom left), 112, 116, 117, 121 (all three pictures), 123 (both pictures), 138, 141
© **Jerry Hennen:** Pages 2, 19 (left and bottom right)
© **James P. Rowan:** Pages 6, 120
Root Resources: © Bill Thomas: Pages 8-9; © Art Brown: Page 20 (bottom right); © Charlene Faris: Page 83
© **Virginia Grimes:** Page 19 (top right)
© **William Strode:** Pages 20 (top left, middle left, bottom left), 21 (top left, bottom left, bottom right), 23, 50, 55
University of Kentucky: Pages 20 (middle right), 89
The Bettmann Archive: Pages 26, 29, 30 (left), 31, 33, 35, 38 (inset), 43 (left), 44, 47, 49, 67, 85 (left), 129 (Carson), 130 (Lynn), 131 (Stevenson)
Bettmann Newsphotos: Page 57
UPI/Bettmann Archive: Page 129 (Collins)
Kentucky Historical Society: Pages 36, 38-39
The Photo Source: Pages 37 (left), 62, 94 (right); © P. Beney: Page 80
Photri: 43 (bottom right), 57 (left), 83 (right), 110; © Kay Shaw: Page 37 (right); © Leonard Lee Rue: Page 108 (bottom right)
Historical Pictures Service, Inc., Chicago: Pages 41 (both pictures), 127, 128 (Audubon and Breckinridge), 129 (Clark), 130 (Filson), 131 (Rutledge and Shelby)
Wide World Photos: Pages 43 (top right), 48, 58, 128 (Bingham and Brandeis), 129 (Clay), 130 (Lincoln and Morgan), 131 (Rice), 132
University of Louisville Photographic Archives: Page 52
Nawrocki Stock Photo: © R. Perron: Page 72; © Michael Brohm: Pages 75, 90 (inset), 118 (both pictures); © William S. Nawrocki: Page 87 (bottom)
R/C Photo Agency: © J. Madeley: Page 77; © Richard L. Capps: Page 108 (top right)
Louisville Convention and Visitors Bureau: Page 81 (inset)
Greater Lexington Convention and Visitors Bureau: Page 98
© **Reinhard Brucker:** Page 104
Kentucky Department of Travel Development: Page 108 (background picture)
Len W. Meents: Maps on pages 93, 96, 98, 103, 107, 136
Courtesy Flag Research Center, Winchester, Massachusetts 01890: Flag on page 108

About the Author

Sylvia McNair is the author of numerous books for adults and young people about interesting places. A graduate of Oberlin College, she has toured all fifty of the United States and more than thirty foreign countries. Her travels have included many visits to all sections of Kentucky. Always interested in education, she served for six years on a district school board in Illinois. McNair now lives in Evanston, Illinois. She has three sons, one daughter, and two grandsons.

DATE DUE

Litho
0452

976.9	McNair, Sylvia
MCN	America the beautiful.
	Kentucky

DATE DUE	BORROWER'S NAME	

976.9	McNair, Sylvia
MCN	America the beautiful.
	Kentucky